THE
TROUT FISHER'S
HANDBOOK

THE
TROUT FISHER'S
HANDBOOK

LESLEY CRAWFORD

SWAN·HILL
PRESS

Other books by Lesley Crawford

Scotland's Classic Wild Trout Waters Swan Hill Press, 2000

Fishing for Wild Trout in Scottish Lochs Swan Hill Press, 1996

An Angler's Year in Caithness and Sutherland Northern Times, 1992

Caithness and Sutherland, Trout Loch Country North of Scotland
Newspapers, 1991

Copyright ©2002 Lesley Crawford
First published in the UK in 2002 by Swan Hill Press,
an imprint of Quiller Publishing Ltd.

British Library Cataloguing-in-Publication Data
A catalogue record for this book
is available from the British Library

ISBN 1 904057 02 0

Printed in Italy

Swan Hill Press
an imprint of Quiller Publishing Ltd.
Wykey House, Wykey, Shrewsbury, SY4 1JA, England
Tel: 01939 261616 Fax: 01939 261606
E-mail: info@quillerbooks.com
Website: www.swanhillbooks.com

DEDICATION
To Ronnie with love

Acknowledgements

I thank the following persons for their kind assistance during the writing of this book: Geoffrey Bucknall, Ron Crawford, Andrew Johnston, Diane Loughborough, Jamie MacGregor, Andy Walker. I also thank Hugh Tunn Jnr, Ewan Crawford and Niall Ross.

Contents

PART 2

INTRODUCTION

My experiences working as a fishing guide in 'God's fishing country', Caithness and Sutherland, have brought to light many queries on how best to fish for wild trout. Time and time again I listen to similar though not identical questions concerning the underwater activities of our much beloved quarry. What are they taking? Where are the fish? Why did I miss him? How do you know they prefer a Soldier Palmer to a Partridge & Orange? You are probably only too well aware of the kind of interrogation I can receive and if truth be told, I sometimes ask myself comparable questions when the trout are playing hard to get! Whilst I always enjoy helping visiting anglers explore unchartered waters, I have often wished that I could condense these years of practical knowledge into a handbook which could be referred to when I am not standing at your side. The publication of this book has given me the opportunity of doing just that.

The Trout Fisher's Handbook is a practical angling guide written from the sharp end of trout fishing. While you may be forgiven for thinking there are already enough books on the market conveying assorted techniques of catching trout, what hopefully sets this book apart is the presentation of ideas predominantly from a wild fish standpoint. Rather like my approach to trying to catch trout out on a gale-blasted heath, there is no room here for waffle. Hence much of the chapter layout is sharp and easily read being designed to cover most aspects of the physical pursuit of trout in essentially wild places. There are plenty of nuggets of tactical information on everything from fishing the small stillwater to the big lake and from tackling the wide river to the narrow stream. I also try to answer many of trout fishing's most frequently asked questions. The book's essence revolves around carefully selected 'tricks of the trade' along with insider views, conservation hints and fact and fiction scenarios. At the end of each chapter there is a 'top tips' section which acts as an affirmation of what has gone before. Do not hesitate to make use of these quick summaries especially if the rain's horizontal and the wind's blowing daggers in your face!

I have attempted to look at most aspects of how to fish for wild trout in fine detail while striking a balance between the obvious and the more unusual, rather like fish behaviour in fact. Yes, you will find lots of hard fact information on tackle and tactics for selected venues but equally there are important chapters on topics such as introducing youngsters to fishing; our siblings are after all the future of the sport. I have pondered past masters, looked at the mysteries of today's trout angler, dissected successful casting, mused on fly tying skills and contemplated tackle requirements. My aim has always been to keep it concise and to the point. The target audience could be said to be beginners to intermediate skilled anglers but believe me, there is something here for all with an interest in catching trout.

Those of you who have read *Scotland's Classic Wild Trout Waters* and/or *Fishing for Wild Trout in Scottish Lochs* will know that my enthusiasm for trout shows no signs of diminishing. With this book I want to bring into precise relief the down to earth practicalities of it all while continuing to emphasise both the positive and the ethereal. My ultimate goal is to set you off on the long road to becoming the perfect fly fisher however this is not simply a clinical dissection of angling techniques. To write it that way would be like trying to deprive trout of their essential mystery, an impossible task when no one can ever know every-thing there is to know about fishing for them. Instead I want to bring a more rounded approach to your fishing emphasising as much the therapeutic benefits as the hard nosed realities. Trout are enigmatic, unpredictable and challenging creatures and long may they stay that way. This work is therefore about encour-agement, shedding light on ideas old and new and building on the basics whilst keeping things in reasonable perspective. Your experiences in this type of angling should be joyful and full of fun as much as they are concerned with trying to unravel the sport's many mysteries. Above all your fishing should bring you many cherished memories.

Remember the sheer electric thrill you experienced when you first succeeded in capturing a trout; the spark that lit the flame of a life long passion. That is the type of dynamic enthusiasm I want to bring to this work and I write with that glow ever uppermost in mind. Forget any sanitised clinical textbook approach, this is practical wild trout angling dissected but celebrated all at the same time. There is and always will be a heady and compelling attraction about going fishing for those speckled beauties wherever they reside. So what are we waiting for?

PART 1

1
WHAT'S NEW IN TROUT FISHING?

'If I have seen farther it is by standing on the shoulders of giants'
Sir Isaac Newton

THE DEVELOPMENT OF TROUT FLY FISHING

Is there anything really innovative in today's trout fishing? The answer to that question is to put it bluntly, probably no. In terms of equipment we have advanced a long way from the days of greenheart rods, silk lines and horse-hair casts, however many of our most favoured modern techniques have their roots set in the fifteenth century or even earlier. The art of **wet fly** fishing is the oldest form of angling. It began aeons ago and was for centuries thought to be the only type of fly fishing skill required to catch trout. The earliest record of casting a fly goes right back to Roman times when in the third century AD, Aelian wrote of fishing with a fly of red wool and feathers for a 'spotted fish' (almost certainly trout) on a nearby stream. It is believed Aelian had tied this fly to represent a local insect of the period however it would be nice to think that with this dressing he may have created the forerunner to the Soldier Palmer series.

Thereafter an assortment of references appear on wet fly fishing for trout. The ground breaking *Treatise of Fishing with an Angle* was published in 1420 and in this work, attributed to Dame Juliana Berners, there are clear instructions on how to tie a selection of timeless classic wet fly patterns. The angler was very much encouraged to fish flies according to the seasons with a selection noted for each month of the year. The wet fly cause was then much furthered during the 1600s by Walton, Cotton and Colonel Venables. These fellows further laid down the foundations of the wet fly techniques propounded in the *Treatise*. In fishing wet fly today we may use different more sophisticated tackle and have more exact scientific knowledge of entomology but when you get right down to it the basic theory has not changed that much.

It is interesting to see that, despite its long accepted status, the **dry fly** was only added to the fishers' armoury in the early nineteenth century. Though there are some oblique references to 'floating flies' made in earlier times, the cult of dry fly has its roots in the 1800s. J. W. Hills in *A History of Fly Fishing for Trout* details angling writers like Mascall of the sixteenth century discussing flies which 'floateth best' and how they were fished 'aloft on the water'. Hills debates whether these were actual dry patterns – he thought they were flies fished just below the surface in the current. More likely I feel the anglers of old had little

Dry fly was only added to the fishers' armoury in the early nineteenth century

choice but to fish out the fly as it fell on the water; if it sank or floated that's how they fished it. Whatever its origins, angling with dry fly had really taken off by the mid 1800s. Francis Francis in *A Book on Angling* published around 1867 declared the dry fly to be in widespread use in the south with its use growing throughout the land. However it was the legendary Frederic M. Halford circa 1886 who really managed to drive the dry fly to cult, and at times snobbish, status. With his highly analytical and occasionally dogmatic prose Halford was partly responsible for a considerable amount of unnecessary elitism creeping into the art of fly fishing. We must not be too critical of FMH however, remember his followers were willing and often pushy accomplices who may well have elevated dry fly doctrine to its lofty standing in an attempt to further their own conceits.

The use of the **nymph** came into fashion almost as a backlash to the pretentiousness of dry fly angling. Though it has to be said nymph fishing is just another form of wet fly angling, a fair degree of mystique grew up around its use particularly on rivers. The main proponents of latter day 'nymphing', as opposed to styles seen on rainbow trout fisheries today, included the famous G. M. Skues during the 1920s. The use of upstream nymphs was, however, well established in Scotland by the time Skues wrote his then daring dissertation of the 1920s. W. C. Stewart had graphically described using upstream 'Spiders' (nymphs by any other name) some sixty years earlier, but it is Skues who undoubtedly gets most of the nymphing credit. Skues was an exceptionally gifted writer and expertly quantified the worth of casting an upstream nymph to a rising trout. Despite the claims of his detractors, Skues did not actually declare his style of nymph fishing to be the only way to catch fish, rather he thought it should be used as one method in the armoury employed along with dry or wet as conditions dictated. Unfortunately the nouveau dry fly 'purists' of the Shires went off at a tangent when hearing of Skues' theories pronouncing his concepts heretical and blasphemous in the face of the Halford upstream dry doctrine!

It is obvious even from this short examination of the development of styles for dry, wet or nymph fishing that the course of trout fishing history has been one of slow evolution, less obvious is the fact that it was frequently laced with controversial argument. Even in devising basic methods of fishing for trout many questions were raised and often vociferously disputed. How dare those fellows use something different from me? But wait a minute, is it better? Shall I now change to upstream dry or continue with downstream wet? Will I be criticised either way? What's this upstream nymph supposed to do? Can it be compared to traditional methods? The debates on tactics were long and fierce and often verging on pure rhetoric: however sensible discussion and reasoned argument laid the baseline for how we fish today. All in all if you were a past master in those heady developing days, considerable skill and a thick skin were definite prerequisites!

Let us now examine in detail some of the tactics used by the more influential doyens of trout fishing and look at how we can apply their ideas today...

PAST TROUT MASTERS
Dame Juliana Berners – circa 1496

We have no real way of knowing whether this venerable lady was a supreme angling master or not for though her name is forever associated with the corner-stone book *Treatise of Fishing with an Angle* it is now thought she is but one of a number of contributors to this tome and that the book was a compilation of earlier works. However authorship is somewhat academic for what she and/or others recorded, laid the foundations of trout angling as we now know it. Much of what the *Treatise* propounded is still useful five hundred plus years on. Take rods for example – '*It (the rod) will be light and full nimble to fish with*' simple advice and I wish some modern manufacturers followed it! Well used maxims like '*when you hook a fish be not in a hurry to land him*', '*keep your shadow off the water*', '*strike not too slow nor too quick*', '*choose a whirling water*', '*fish early and late (in the day) from May to September*' all appear, indeed it is likely these nuggets are accumulated knowledge from a good deal earlier.

Perhaps the most famous gems from the *Treatise* are the selection of flies to be fished according to the time of year. Many claim these dozen or so tyings can be recognised in modern wet patterns; the twenty-first century February Red for example is the Dun Fly of old, while our modern day Alder Fly pattern bears very close resemblance to Berners' ancient Drake Fly. However the key importance

'Choose a whirling water'

of the *Treatise* patterns is not so much what they resemble today as the fact that they were all tied to match a hatch by colour and shape. The *Treatise* mentions inspecting the contents of the trout's stomach to see what the catch has been feeding on. Thus 'spooning' trout is an extremely old practice and not at all what some modern reservoir pundits would have us believe.

Another interesting point to come from the *Treatise* is the method of '*showing the butt*' to a heavy fish. Today 'giving the fish butt' if you will pardon the expression, is thought to be applying hearty pressure to a fish in order to control it. Wrong – showing the butt to a fish was actually a method of playing a trout delicately by lofting the rod over your shoulder and pointing the butt end at the quarry so as to make full use of the rod's flexibility. Funny how we can switch history around to suit our aims...

Isaak Walton and Charles Cotton – circa 1676

I mention these two past greats in the same breath for both made huge contributions to angling history by writing editions of that famous book *The Compleat Angler*. Unquestionably Walton and Cotton pushed angling knowledge to new heights, building on the information contained in the *Treatise*, rounding off some of its rougher edges and putting in new dimensions of their own. They wrote in differing styles however, with Walton the lyrical philosopher and Cotton the more thoughtful tactician. Walton emphasised the importance of natural representation of insects in fly tying à la *Treatise*, with his fly selection including patterns such as the Dun Fly, Stone Fly, Dark Drake, Yellow Fly, Black Fly and the Shell Fly. These are the 'foundation' patterns of fly fishing and most modern day tyings are derived from these designs.

A number of new developments occurred in this era including the use of a reel with the rod. Before then the line was simply attached to the rod end by means of a loop of horsehair. Walton records using a reel for salmon angling in 1655 and though he did not invent 'winders' or 'winches' (reels) he certainly had a hand in pioneering their use for trout fishing in the UK albeit with some caution. We also have to thank Walton for the inspiring axiom '*I am Sir, a Brother of the Angle*' – a phrase rarely bettered when it comes to summing up the bonds which hold us together in this unique sport.

Charles Cotton extended the fly tyers' repertoire considerably mentioning some sixty-five original dressings for trout flies. He was something of an entomologist giving a pretty accurate account of the habits of stone flies describing the bottom crawling of the fat stonefly nymph and detailing a fine pattern for imitating the winged insect. While Cotton was an avid follower of the school of matching the hatch he also had some '*fancy flies*' (general representations) up his sleeve including hackled flies and flies with a 'silver twist'. He was keen on stalking fish and imitative angling, the well known phrase fishing '*fine and far off*' comes from him, and he thought that if you could not see what the trout were taking you should try a '*small hackle*', presumably a sparse nymph type imitation. Cotton was not a purist in the strictest sense however for it is he who is credited with inventing clear water upstream worming, itself a difficult art to master. Equally he adhered more to casting a fly according to which way the wind blew rather than plumping solely for downstream or upstream. Sensible advice then and now!

Robert Venables – 1612-1687

Though perhaps not as well known as his contemporaries Walton and Cotton, Colonel Venables wrote a remarkably plain talking book on fishing entitled *The Experienced Angler*. Venables was a redoubtable soldier who during his colourful life fought under the Cromwell regime, sailed overseas to secure lands for King and country and spent time in the Tower of London for failing in that bid! He was however considerably more successful in his angling efforts.

Venables' ideas were well ahead of his time and he was one of the first to write about fishing upstream with wet fly rather than across and down. He also questioned the established theory of rigidly using a certain fly for a certain month. Instead he thought one should adapt the type of fly used to a) the local hatch at the time and b) the local environmental conditions. '*I have observed that several rivers and soils produce several sorts of flies*' he stated thus putting a new perspective on the fifteenth century *Treatise* which recommended a distinctly seasonal fly choice. Equally he had a grasp of the practicalities of angling for example he thought that when you try and '*fit your colour to the fly*' i.e. match the hatch you must '*wet your fur, hair, wool or moccado, otherwise you will fail in your work*' – remember flies would be tied in hand at the water's edge then. Wetting of the materials he argued gave a more realistic colour match between natural and artificial.

Venables quotes those old gems '*In dark weather as well as dark waters, your fly must be dark*' and also '*If the day be clear, then (use) a light coloured fly with slender body and wings*'. He does not attribute these sayings to anyone so its obvious that even if he did not write them personally, these pieces of sensible advice were around since time immemorial. I was also pleased to see that he cites the catholic diet of trout as being all sorts of worms, many different flies, minnows, cad bait (caddis), wasps, bees, caterpillars, grasshoppers and small frogs. No messing with the pretensions of dry fly only here. Venables also mentions that trout consume gentles, cankers, bark worm, dores, bobs (possibly a type of maggot), marsh worms and palmers. Since today we are unlikely to know what these are, except for the palmer which was believed to be a type of caterpillar and was the forerunner for palmered artificial flies, we will have to take his word on that.

'*When you angle for trout you need not make above three or four trials in one place*'

Probably one of his most astute observations is that *'when you angle for trout, you need not make above three or four trials in the one place ... you lose time to stay there any longer'*. Nearly four hundred years later I frequently find myself saying the same thing to beginners, especially novices brought up on a diet of stocked rainbow trout given to swimming conveniently past the static bank angler.

Thomas T. Stoddart – 1810-1880

Though there were a few angling notables during the 1700s – Bowlker, Howlett and Saunders amongst them – for some reason it is not until the nineteenth century that trout angling tactics take another significant leap forward. In Scotland in particular, Thomas Stoddart undoubtedly had a considerable hand in popularising the sport. Stoddart was a river as opposed to loch trout enthusiast spending much of his life fishing the Border streams. He was a prolific angler who fished with an obsessive zeal and he had little time for those who questioned what he was about. The short sharp exchange between himself and a friend who dared to ask what he was doing – *'Doing? Man, I am an Angler!'* – is well documented. His inspiring yet practical books on fishing notably *Anglers Companion to Rivers and Lochs of Scotland* and *The Scottish Angler* both written in the 1830-1840 period added another foundation stone in trout fishing writing.

While Stoddart is not seen as an inventor of new techniques for trout he was well able to record the tactics of the period. He practised a traditional wet fly across and down approach using a switch cast, was seen to use some false casting techniques and had very firm ideas on fly selection. Unlike others of this century Stoddart did not believe trout were attracted to flies because of their exact dressing i.e. because you matched the hatch. Instead he felt the fish were more likely to take patterns because of their *'size, motion, form and colour'*. Stoddart went further in one of his books and radically simplified his fly choice to patterns featuring black, red or brown hackles (presumably with different coloured bodies), and also advocated the Hare Lug fly, a version of the Hare's Ear Nymph of today. Quite why he did this is unclear for it is noted elsewhere that he used many more flies than just a few stark choices. One thing is certain though, Stoddart favoured sparsely dressed dull coloured flies above all else to catch trout. His disgust at the *'gaudy fly'* (brightly dressed 'lure' type trout flies originating from salmon fly design) used in the Highlands and indeed for all things of Gaelic origin is much recorded.

Stoddart may not have written highly technical doctrines but his lyrical and passionate descriptions of his beloved trout angling mean he must receive considerable credit for encouraging many more into the sport of angling in Scotland.

W. C. Stewart – circa 1850

Sadly W. C. Stewart did not live beyond the age of forty yet his information-packed book *The Practical Angler*, published in 1857 and revised and reprinted no less than sixteen times, laid the baseline for many other books on the subject. His crisp erudite writing style meant he was able to convey his fishing techniques in some considerable detail. Like his Scottish contemporary Stoddart, Stewart spent most of his time fishing Scottish Border rivers such as the Tweed, Nith and Annan. Though he did do some loch/lake fishing he was essentially a river trout fanatic. Stewart was a devoted follower of using sparse flies and on that Stewart and Stoddart firmly agreed. Unfortunately they appear to agree on little else. Verbal swords were frequently crossed over many of the finer points for example whether one should try and match artificial to the real thing (Stewart thought so, Stoddart did not), whether clear water worming was a more difficult art than fly fishing (Stoddart thought this, Stewart disagreed) and whether it was necessary to cast flies upstream (Stewart) or simply go across (Stoddart).

Stewart is often accredited as being a pioneer of upstream wet fly however the anglers of the seventeenth century had already propounded this technique. Equally his famously sparse fly dressings commonly known as 'Spiders', are now thought to be adaptations of old North Country patterns made better to suit his own particular needs. Certainly he mentions that the Black Spider was *'first shown to him by James Baillie'* a renowned angler of that era, so there does seem to have been some reworking going on. Nevertheless Stewart was no charlatan angler and his skills are still highly noteworthy. He gives a lovely description of how to tie Spiders 'in hand' i.e. without the aid of a vice – *'still holding the hook between forefinger and thumb of your left hand, take the thread, lay it along the centre of the inside of the feather and with your right hand twirl them round together til the feather is rolled round the thread...'* I wonder how many of us could do this now without the aid of contemporary equipment.

Stewart's tactical advice on fishing for trout is astute and cannot be bettered today. *'We advise the angler who is using a long line, and raising but not hooking trout, to shorten his line, and he will at once be struck by the difference.'* *'When the flies are just about alighting on the water, you should slightly raise the point of your rod; this checks their downward motion, and they fall much more softly.'* *'The moment the fly alights being the most deadly of the whole cast.'* These are all sensible pieces of advice and just as relevant today as they were in the 1800s.

Sadly the fact that Stewart wrote about Scottish trout almost as if the trout of England were a different species, meant that he did not receive quite the nationwide credit he actually deserved. Old rivalries between the two countries saw to that – some things never change!

Three Anglers – circa 1888

While the anonymity of 'Three Anglers' may seem odd in this egotistical age (actually they were all Edinburgh based medics and the book they compiled together could easily have been written by Three Doctors) there was nothing

'The moment the fly alights being the most deadly of the whole cast'

vague about their exceptionally useful field guide entitled quite simply *How to Catch Trout*. They were firm believers in the 'always upstream' Stewart doctrine and placed great significance on using sparse patterns. However they did advance the fly tying theories of the age slightly by acknowledging *'Early in the season ... a heavier body is often advantageous, and this ... can be made of hare lug, water rat or mole's furs, floss silk or mohair wool'*. This was progress on the fashion for ultra skinny patterns of the period. Equally they recognised the value of adjusting methods up or downstream to suit the prevailing conditions rather than simply following dogma.

The Three Anglers also gave astute advice on times of fishing for example early and late in the season they suggest the warmest parts of the day between 11am to 2pm, while in summer conditions they suggested fishing the early and late half of the day. Though they derided stillwater (loch) trout fishing as not as skilful as river angling, they nevertheless gave sound traditional advice as to how to go about it! *'In cloudy weather, or when trout are feeding freely on the surface dull coloured flies imitating the natural insect may generally be used... in bright weather silver bodied flies such as the Butcher are often successful.'* Similarly they showed a sound grasp of the fundamentals of 'loch style' advocating keeping the wet flies moving on or just below the surface in the traditional way. When bank angling they advised taking a step along between each cast to avoid fishing the same water.

Their description of dry fly angling is worth repetition here for it is spiked with wry humour. The Three Anglers thought dry fly the easiest way of catching trout, decidedly less hard work and the method most suited to *'the nature of the mature elderly angler'* – I wonder what the Halford camp thought of that!

F. M. Halford – circa 1886

Though Halford did not invent floating/dry fly tactics his name is synonymous with its practice. He firmly believed a carefully selected natural looking upstream dry fly delicately cast over a stalked rising trout was *the* way to catch fish and few of us would argue with that. However where he, or more likely his fanatical followers, went a bit askew was in proclaiming it as the *only* way to catch fish, which of course is incorrect. Also because Halford wrote about his experiences of dry fly angling on chalk streams the unfortunate correlation was made by others that dry fly could not be practised anywhere else other than a limpid limestone stream. This is now known to be quite wrong though it never ceases to amaze me the number of quizzical looks I get when I recommend dry fly on a wild Highland loch. And this is the twenty-first century!

Nevertheless Halford's fly designs were both beautiful and elegant. His Detached-Bodied May Fly has never been bettered and though one could argue that it may have been adapted from a tying made before his time, the Halford patterns are nevertheless exquisite. His methods may not always be right for every angling situation but Halford added a new dimension to angling and we have much to thank him for...

The Marquess of Granby and others – circa 1898

In *The Trout* published as part of the Fur, Feather & Fin Series, the redoubtable Marquess brought together many of the late nineteenth century ideas on trout natural history and trout angling. He was a recorder more than an innovator but he still had some astute things to say. Though there may have been others before, he is one of the first past masters I have found who refers to '*chuck and chance it*'. Naturally this was to point out that this was an inferior method of fishing when compared with upstream dry though at least he qualifies that by saying '*dry fly can only be followed under certain conditions*'. The Marquess advocated a calm unhurried approach to his fishing stating that '*hurry is most undesirable when beginning a day's fishing*' and highlighted the necessity of a good recce of the river before starting.

Despite the Marquess's flowery Victorian prose there are important snippets including the necessity of casting a short line first to search the shallows rather than casting into infinity first go. He also attempted to explain different trout feeding patterns as in '*bulging*', '*tailing*' or '*rising*' mode. He recommended using palmered flies, Spiders or even Zulus for tailing (predominantly shrimp feeding) trout while employing winged flies for rising fish. However he rather baulked at bulging fish declaring them as very difficult to attract. Strangely he does not go into nymph fishing as a method of catching them however it can be argued that Skues was yet to write his nymph bible! There is also some interesting material on hatched mayflies including the fact that trout will sometimes '*hit it (*a mayfly*) with their noses and retire swiftly*'. This form of behaviour the Marquess quaintly puts down to a '*temporary form of indigestion*' or simply

'prospecting' by the trout. Though today we now think the trout are trying to stun or drown the mayfly before engulfing it the fact that the Marquess recorded this type of trout behaviour shows that angler's observational powers had continued to develop and expand.

Above all else *The Trout* excels in its recording of the era's methods of trout rearing and breeding. Several chapters written by a Colonel Custance are included and much thought-provoking theory is put forward on the history of stocking including the symbiotic relationship between fishery and hatchery owners. We can see that by the 1890s the unintentional destruction of existing native trout stocks by strain dilution was already well and truly underway in the UK. Restocking was rampant by the end of the nineteenth century with all consideration given to angler's sport and little if any thought given to the loss of genetically intact strains of trout (see Chapter 6).

G. M. Skues – circa 1910

Skues is best described as an innovator in the Halford mould though they were considered to be poles apart in their doctrine. His book *The Way of a Trout with a Fly* first published in 1921 boldly analysed the natural feeding of trout in rivers. Before Skues the essence of fishing had become dominated by dry fly purism and the need to present an exact imitation upstream only to a visibly rising trout. Skues questioned the necessity of always fishing the upstream dry and advocated using upstream nymphs as another way of catching trout particularly in difficult 'glassy smooth' or windy conditions and/or when trout were steadfastly refusing surface imitations.

Above all Skues was an astute observer and his descriptions of types of trout rises have stood the test of time. He differentiated between sipping rises to small floating duns, midges and spinners and slashing rises to sedge and also noted head and tail rises to wet duns, bulging to nymphs, the sucking rise to medium-sized floating flies and the big rise with a kidney-shaped whorl to floating duns. Skues also observed the purpose behind a trout taking a fly for example out of *'hunger, curiosity, rapacity or tyranny'*. Though these adroit descriptions may well have been uttered well before Skues, his is the first record I can find of such exact descriptions of trout feeding behaviour.

W. Earl Hodgson – circa 1920

Hodgson may not have achieved quite the fame Skues did in the early 1900s but his book *Trout Fishing* is worthy of recognition. Though technically it did not break any new ground it still contains some gems of angling information. Rather than telling us 'how to do it' as so many of his peers did, Hodgson took a different tack and stuck to detailing various reasons why we fail to catch trout! He wrote lyrically on the annoying effects of changes in temperature, wind direction, barometric pressure and the amount of light on the water surface. There is an intriguing theory put forward about *'lanes of light'* being disruptive to trout fishing, Hodgson certainly thought they had a detrimental effect in causing the fish not to see so well. He also had little time for the concept of *'educated'* trout (see also Chapter 6) believing that fish have very little in the way of cognitive cunning rather they just took flies as a feeding response.

This book is also highly memorable for a rather good malapropism which runs like this; *'Seeing that the fly on the water was a small insect with greyish white wings and a black body, I put on a cast of midgets, rowed out to the middle of the loch, and had very good sport indeed'*. A cast of 'midgets' or 'midgettes'. Hmm, could be a great name for small midge imitations...

T. C. Kingsmill Moore – 1960

I was still getting to grips with primary school when Kingsmill Moore wrote his milestone book *A Man May Fish* and only came to it much later in life. I am thankful I did though for this book must be regarded as one of the most influential on modern fly tying techniques particularly when constructing flies for stillwater fishing. Kingsmill Moore was a highly thoughtful writer who eloquently rationalised his skills in making trout patterns, his chapter on 'The Choice of Flies' should be compulsory reading for those of us obsessed with carting around boxes upon boxes of patterns, most of which we rarely use. He put forward a number of simple yet astute theories about tying flies including the idea that flies should be tied using colours resembling the water base where they are to be used. He also said that flies should be made to trap varying amounts of light and air within their hackles as he thought these factors played a significant part in how they eventually might attract a waiting trout (see Chapter 8). Kingsmill appreciated the theory that trout recognise their prey by the way it moves and all his fly tying led on from that. He believed that flies should also be tied to move through the water in a natural life-like way. His famous tyings of old North Country 'Bumbles' notably the Claret Bumble and the Golden Olive Bumble are now standards for loch fishing everywhere.

With Kingsmill Moore I shall leave the masters of trout angling. Though numerous notable fishers and fishing writers have emerged since those heady formative days it has to be said that many of today's angling methods simply recreate, rework or reapply ancient well established customs. We may think we are doing something entirely new and novel but in actual fact it has probably all been done many times before. However do not let the fact that we are revisiting old traditions detract from the unique learning process that is trout fishing. As you go about developing your trout angling skills remember it is all importantly fresh and exciting to you and when you get right down to it, that is all that matters – *'Angling is a science which can never be fully learnt'* said Walton and who can quibble with that…

TROUTFISHER'S SELECTED TOP TIPS FROM PAST MASTERS

1. *'A dark lowering day with a whistling wind, or with a soft wind, are both good.'* (Dame Juliana Berners 1496.) Even in the fifteenth century anglers' obsessions with the weather are clearly in evidence. This advice is as good today as its always been.

2. *'Be sure in casting, that your fly falls first into the water, for if the line fall first, it scares or frightens the fish.'* (Colonel Venables 1662.) Refers more to precision of presentation with ancient horsehair line and cast as opposed to modern day techniques, but delicacy in casting in any situation remains important.

3 *'To fish fine and far off is the first and principal rule for trout angling.'* (Charles Cotton 1676.) Again this refers to the significance of a delicate touch when presenting flies to trout but 'fine and far off' is still a common and important maxim in the fishing vernacular.

4 *'When wind lanes are strictly marginal, they exercise an attractive power over fish, disposing them to look out for surface food and approach the water's edge for this purpose.'* (T. Stoddart 1866.) Refers to 'slick' wind lanes sometimes seen just offshore on large stillwaters rather than those gale blown streaks of foam which appear on lochs in high winds. Still very applicable today.

5 *'Although it is impossible to strike too soon, it is quite possible to strike too hard.'* (W. C. Stewart 1857.) Needs no further explanation and is wise counsel for a wild fish even though Dame Juliana said something similar three hundred and fifty years earlier!

6 *'Where to catch trout – what a trout likes is just a lazy man's idea of paradise; too much to eat, too little to do, and safety.'* (Three Anglers 1888.) Nowadays we might revise that to: too much to eat, too little to do, sex at the appropriate time and safety – but the principal's just the same.

7 *'Before the first cast is made it may be worthwhile to mark carefully the peculiarities of the water wherein are the rising trout.'* (Marquess of Granby 1898.) The value of a good recce by any other name.

8 *'In nature nothing happens without a reason.'* (G. M. Skues 1921.) Skues is referring to the vagaries of trout behaviour and the fact that though it may be obvious to trout what they are about, it is not always so obvious to the angler trying to catch him.

9. *'Even if we could lie under water and look upwards, we could have no assurance that our vision of things would be identical with that of a trout.'* (Earl Hodgson 1920.) Needs no further comment.

10. *'Speaking broadly, surface life is translucent and sub surface life is opaque.'* (Kingsmill Moore 1960.) Refers to the properties of flies fished on the surface as having light coming through the hackles whereas sunk/wet flies reflect light and appear more solid. Important to consider when fly tying.

'In nature nothing happens without a reason' G.M. Skues

2

TODAY'S TROUT ANGLER

'Talents are best nurtured in solitude, character is best formed in the stormy billows of the world'
Goethe

WHY WE FISH

Trout angling is such a unique pastime involving many different senses and it is actually rather difficult to describe just why we do it. Some of us go simply for the escape that fishing offers from our demanding busy lives and undoubtedly the 'feel good' factor of open water, fresh air and sociable or solitary exercise has a powerful attraction. Others want to fish purely for the challenge relishing the degree of difficulty in winkling out trout from problematical waters. Both the escapist and the seeker of enlightenment will share in common the thrill of anticipation experienced before and during angling. John Buchan described the charm of fishing as *'the pursuit of what is elusive but obtainable, a perpetual series of occasions of hope'*. To me that description has no equal. It sums up exactly why we go, to enjoy a risky business while sharpening our skills and enjoying a day out in a different scenic environment.

The quintessential attraction of wild trout angling is therefore its degree of uncertainty. Brownies rarely if ever play by our rules. When fishing for trout you are the outsider trying to enter and make sense of a wild creature's instinct dominated world. This is the principal test of trout angling and without this edge of unpredictability it could never be as enjoyable. No one can ever attain full knowledge of how to fish for wild trout for the fish have such a challenging nature they can make fools of any 'expert' at any time. The quest for this knowledge is an integral part of trout fishing's enjoyment. Angling for a wild, naturally reproducing fish in an uncultivated, or at least semi untamed place, is a great leveller. Unlike the situation where money can buy access to the best salmon fishing beats thereby usually assisting the catch rate, trout just cannot be bought. Kings and commoners may fish for browns and the outcome will be the same, some will catch and some won't!

To become a consistently successful angler you have to put together a number of building blocks which start at the basics of wielding the rod and progress from there. You will find that once fishing gets in the blood you embark on a long learning curve, one that is rarely if ever completed. For example casting skills have to be complemented by an ability to read the water to ascertain where the

The quintessential attraction of trout angling is its degree of uncertainty

fish are and what they are feeding on. Success is seldom instantly achieved. The joy of the sport unfolds over a considerable but pleasurable length of time. I have always had the firm belief that angling is a lifelong hobby to be relished from the short kid in wellies with a plastic net on the end of a cane, right through to dotage. I may not be the wise old arthritic grey haired sage yet but then I'm not the wide eyed wet behind the ears bairn either, just somewhere in between!

GETTING STARTED

Trout fishermen today come in all shapes, sizes and abilities. We range from the occasional tourist who fishes only in the holidays to the fanatic who is out virtually every day barring illness or necessities like work or family. If you are relatively new to trouting you will quickly come to realise there are a variety of choices to be made. Initially you may see yourself becoming a loch/lake angler or perhaps a small river fisher but there are other facets to the sport which you must consider. To ease your rite of passage here are some of the questions you should ask yourself...

What do you want from your angling? This is the principal question to consider for around it all other decisions are made. Your expectations are paramount. Do you want lots of mixed trout fishing in a variety of lakes, lochs and streams (I wish) or do you simply want the occasional visit to a pleasant scenic spot to fish, relax and get away from it all? Is catching fish the vital requirement of your fishing outings, or are you happy with different tranquil surroundings where a wild trout is a bonus but not a constant necessity?

What are your constraints? For most of us it is time. Busy jobs and hectic family life often mean much less time can be spent fishing than we would like. Travel time to and from an angling haunt may also be a limitation. On the other hand if you are newly retired it may mean you have little in the way of restrictions and can go at it full tilt.

Location is important

Where am I likely to be predominantly fishing? Location is important. Are you near easily accessible trout water or will you have to spend hours in the car travelling to a suitable venue? Do you have the type of fishing you want nearby for example the big reservoir or a small stream, or do you have a lengthy drive to reach it? Time is a vital resource which modern society has less and less of and whether you like it or not, it will always affect your angling.

What kind of skill level are you aiming for? Do you want deeply challenging cerebral stuff or do you simply want undemanding fishing with a fair chance of catching something without too much brainstorming effort? Note however that you will find skill level requirements often change as you become more accomplished and what was fine in the beginning may not be so later on.

How much can I afford? For those on a tight budget, costs of angling are important. Though trouting is not normally as expensive as salmon fishing there will still be tickets to pay, boats and engines to hire, rod licences (in England only), supplementary or new tackle and so on. 'Spend according to intended use' might be a wise motto.

Do you have any physical restraints? A full eight hour day of fishing especially in mountain goat country can knacker even the fittest so choose your fishing carefully. Equally you might prefer to sit in a boat rather than bank fish as the old pins may not be up to slogging around the pond all day!

How you answer these few questions (and being truthful with yourself helps) will determine how your fishing career progresses. If you find the actual logistics like finding instruction or fishing difficult then advice on angling availability is on hand from a number of sources including tackle shops, local water authorities, various angling guidebooks and magazines, the Salmon & Trout Association and The Scottish Anglers National Association. All you need really do is get out there and enjoy it.

WHO WE ARE

Once you are out there throwing a line with the best of them you will begin to develop your own fishing identity. As your career progresses your angling individuality will change and remould itself often for the better. Those around you will also influence you to a certain degree for it is unavoidable that you will encounter a multitude of fishing personas. I thought it might be fun to list just a few of the many types of angler you might meet on the bank and though this list is written in light hearted vein, you would be surprised how many of these fishy types you will actually come across! First up has got to be:

The Fishling

Fishlings are often budding Oracles (see page 34) in the very first flush of youth. Nine times out of ten they are very young and super enthusiastic being barely out of short trousers/ unisex jeans. They hold a clean sheet of angling knowledge and consequently soak up everything you say like the proverbial sponge. Egotists and 'Local Experts' find these youngsters a pain in the neck. As the Fishlings grow older said local experts may even consider them something of a threat. Admittedly a Fishling's searching questions can sometimes leave us wanting to escape their company, however if you remember this type of young angler is becoming thinner and thinner on the ground it is best to put up with, nay encourage, their fervour for trout fishing.

Ewan Crawford – a Fishling if ever there was one

The Deadly Keen

You will always be able to recognise this older version of the Fishling by the way they leap gazelle-like from the car and race to the water leaving a trail of dust in their wake. They are usually the first to arrive at the water, though not always the last to leave. Normally they have little time for contemplative analysis. The rod will be up in a flash and the water whipped to a foam before you can say 'Hugh Falkus'. If they are youthful this angler may well develop into a more rounded character, however should they be in their middle years conversion to higher Oracle ground may be more difficult. Worst habits include asking the same question again and again in slightly different ways and then not really listening to the answer. Better practices include a refreshing determination to absorb all things fishy in as short a time as possible. Often recognised because they wear an ear splitting grin when things are going well and have slumped, stooped shoulders and decidedly glum expression when things are not.

The Sergeant Major

Sergeant Majors tend to be of the older generation and normally have had at some time an association with either the military or the civil service. They do everything in regimented orderly fashion and hate a disruption of routine. Consequently they do not tend to make awfully good anglers as trout fishing is as we know, a delightfully uncertain business. They will often commence battle at 9.30am dead on, stop for lunch exactly at 1pm and leave the water at 5pm precisely, trout rising or not. Sergeant Majors are easily recognised by their deep booming voices when their fishing has been successful and their tendency to stump around red faced and disconsolate when it is not. They often have an air of eccentricity around them but unlike Oracles it is not a welcoming one. Given to back slapping jollity when catching and curt bad humour when not, they show strong tendencies to blame everything and everyone else for their misfortune.

The Duffer

It has to be said that an awful lot of anglers fall into this albeit affable category. Duffers are generally very amiable fishers usually in their mid to late years. They catch quite a few trout but never seem particularly bothered about the need for consistent success. Habits include spending an inordinate amount of time in setting up tackle and selecting an appropriate fly. Alarming back casts which go anywhere from ears to the back of the jacket and losing fly boxes, specs and/or scissors in the long grass are also characteristics. Equally, shutting the rod in a car door or snagging the fly on the back cast just as the only big trout of the day chooses to rise, are notable features. Sometimes they are quite knowledgeable, sometimes they simply make it up as they go along, but they are always pleasant enough company.

The Sloth

Sloths are not the same as Duffers and are the complete opposite to the Sergeant

Majors of our world. They are always late for commencing battle and their appearance is often dishevelled especially if a heavy night has preceded the fishing excursion. Habits include falling asleep in the boat or on the bank, falling into any available water and falling over before or after lunch; in fact they excel at falling down generally. Despite this, Sloths are often quite skilled fishermen capable of catching more than their fair share of trout – usually with a borrowed rod and flies.

The Pest

Pests have the alarming habit of lurking behind trees or walls and then suddenly pouncing on you unawares, usually when you would much rather be alone. They engage you in a continuous loop of conversation asking or giving advice on any topic from line density to what the weather might do. They rarely seem to pause for breath thus making getting away from them exceedingly difficult. Can be any age group from the very young (forgivable) to the very old (not so easy to absolve). It is always advisable to take two aspirin before and after going out in a boat with this one.

The Local Expert

The trouble with trout fishing is that anyone can claim to be an expert however these particular guys should never be confused with Oracles for they are poles apart. Instantly recognisable by their loud voices and the patchwork quilt of badges and flies which adorn the fishing hat, vest or both. Interestingly Local Experts are sometimes given to competition fishing and in extreme cases exhibit habits like taping up their choice of flies with sticky paper so no one else can see them. Often they will talk incessantly about themselves and their latest successes unless what they say might jeopardise the outcome of an angling contest in which case they keep decidedly mum. Easily recognised by the fact they are seriously smug when things have gone well but have gone home early pronouncing the water unfishable if not catching. Their degree of knowledge is sometimes irritatingly good on their local patch but take heart in the fact it can fluctuate wildly if they fish in unfamiliar territory. Often they will be accompanied by Pests who ask them inane questions and pander to their often inflated self-worth. Not all are bad though for young Local Experts who avoid the ego trap often go on to become wise old Oracles, but beware because it is a bit of a lottery.

Tackle Man

This is a breed of angler instantly recognisable by the huge amount of new fishing equipment and accoutrements dangling about his person. Tackle Man dresses in the most up to date angling clothing often at ridiculous expense, has purchased the most costly of rods/reels and lines and has very high expectations of what this tackle can do for his fishing skills. He or she has a high interest in looking good but a low interest in learning about the trout themselves. Habits include wearing fedora hats which blow off (ladies have fedora hats with scarves tied round but they too disappear in high winds). Long lunches and chattering into a mobile phone even when casting have also been seen. Will often drain you dry of local knowledge and then pass it all on to his friends as if he already knew it all. Best avoided unless you feel like grovelling for a loan of their latest piece of kit or possibly a chance to fish the expensive water Tackle Man has just leased.

The Oracle

You will not always know an Oracle from their appearance which is often unassuming and ordinary, it is only when you engage them in conversation that their depth of knowledge will become apparent. These men and women are fountains of wisdom and you should cherish and learn as much as possible from your meetings with them. Sometimes Oracles write books in which case you can carry their hard won expertise with you, but often they do not preferring to quietly fish away haunting a lonely shore. In my 40 odd years of angling I have encountered probably less than ten or these greats so this should give you some idea of their scarcity. Oracles are usually so interesting to speak to, the fishing day will be at least half over before you have had a cast. Habits often include a fair degree of eccentricity and a complete ability to forget the time however there is a degree of quiet self assurance in their fishing which leaves most of us far behind. If you find an Oracle treasure him or her like you would a Sage rod!

***

Oracles often prefer to fish quietly haunting a lonely shore

So ends this light hearted look at who we are and if truth be told, anglers rarely fit exactly into these stereotypes. Normally we show an eclectic mix of a number of these traits so without further ado lets get on with joining the throng.

3

TACKLE CHOICES

'Lightness we consider an essential qualification in a rod'
W. C. Stewart

THE BIG FIVE – ESSENTIAL PIECES OF KIT

There are five essentials which the trout fly fisherman cannot be without and these are rod, reel, line, nylon and flies. They must have a harmonious rather than acrimonious relationship to one another, each item is inextricably linked to the next. Think of the 'Big Five' combination as the vital complementary ingredients in a recipe for successful angling. All other accoutrements are simply add ons to these core elements. Remember that despite what some tackle manufacturers would have us believe, the choice of rod is not necessarily the most critical one you are going to make regarding angling tackle. Yes it must propel line to water but it takes its place in amongst the Big Five rather than at the head of them. Buying a rod is critical but which fly line comes a very close second (think about it for a moment – what comes in closest contact with the trout's watery environment, the rod or the line?!). Equally a reel which encourages hideous memory, nylon which snaps easily or flies that shred after one outing are not going to do anything for you even if your rod cost hundreds of pounds. The Big Five must therefore complement each other fully.

So much has already been written about choosing tackle that I will endeavour not to go over well-trodden ground and instead stick to 'insider'

Tackle choices

tips on selecting your fishing equipment. There are as many lemons out there as there are goodies so let's take a well seasoned look…

TROUTFISHER'S TOP TIPS FOR CHOOSING THE BIG FIVE

Trout Fly Rods

Terminology Butt, reel seat, cork all refer to parts of the handle of the rod. Rod rings, snake rings or guides all refer to the rings placed at intervals along the rod through which the line is threaded. Ferrules are the joints which join the pieces of the rod together. Action or flex is how the rod imparts force to propel the line.

Select a rod suitable to your most popular fishing venue

1 Select a rod which is suitable to where you are most going to use it. Sweet little wands may be great for tiny streams but you might need something a little longer and beefier for the big lakes.

2 Choose one which feels like an extension to your arm, avoid if you can buying a rod 'blind' as it would be a risky business unless you know exactly what you are looking for and even then the advertising blurb may not match the end product.

3 Remember that the rod must fit your physique. There is nothing worse than a rod which is too heavy, light, floppy or stiff for its new owner.

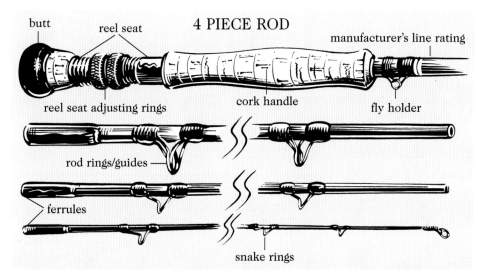

4 PIECE ROD

butt — reel seat — manufacturer's line rating

reel seat adjusting rings — cork handle — fly holder

rod rings/guides

ferrules

snake rings

4 Better tackle shops will have trial areas where you or the intended recipient can cast a practice line. Waggling the rod in the shop will not tell you much, casting with a loaded line does.

5. Quality can usually be judged by the thickness of the rod where it meets the butt cork/reel seat. Thin is normally a sign of fine quality, thick hefty butt sections are often a sign of cheaper range models some (though not all) of which often cast like lemons!

6. Long rods (9ft to 11ft) are recommended for casting long lines in a strong wind, also when your main fishing venue has high banks behind or when you want to work top droppers 'loch style' on the reservoir or loch.

7 Short rods (8ft 6in or less) are good for small waters especially an intimate stream. They are also easier to use in very high winds as their length gives less wind resistance. Children also find short rods less daunting.

8. The action/flex of the rod e.g. 'tip' or 'tip to middle' or 'through' dictates how the rod flexes when you cast. Through action rods can be soft and some find them hard work however they are nice to use from the boat if all you need to do is roll cast and give a well cushioned strike. Tip action rods are a lot stiffer and cast long lines but need good technique both in throwing the line and in striking a fish (I find that with too firm a rod trout can be difficult to hook at long range). Tip to middle action rods are the middle ground in trout fishing and suit most abilities.

9 Rods tend to lose their zip after heavy use and the action can go from semi firm to floppy. The rod's action will alter in character over time and you must make allowances for this unless you have ready cash to replace it.

10 In general terms a sweet light carbon fibre rod of 9ft to 10ft with tip to middle action will do the business almost anywhere for wild trout on river or loch.

Trout Reels

Terminology The drum or arbor is the circular body of the reel which holds the line in place. The spool is the circular removable container holding the line which fits snugly into the drum. Some reels come with extra spools so you can swap from floater to sinker quickly. Drag is the (normally adjustable) amount of pressure exerted on releasing and winding in the line. The drag adjuster is the button or small lever normally on the back of the reel to execute this. The spindle is the central connection between drum and spool.

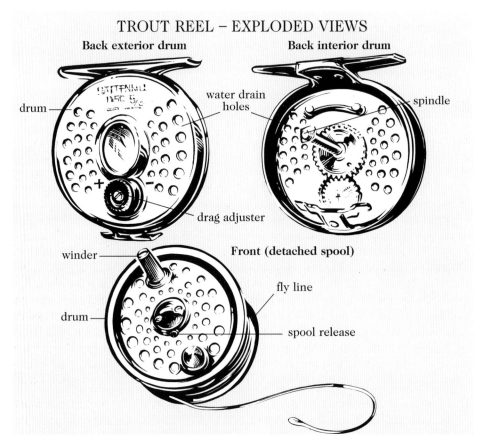

TROUT REEL – EXPLODED VIEWS
Back exterior drum   Back interior drum
drum — water drain holes — spindle — drag adjuster
winder — drum — Front (detached spool) — fly line — spool release

1   Reels should have enough capacity on the drum to store the fly line loosely. Dinky little reels look neat but can corkscrew your line with 'memory' in dramatic fashion. Now that large arbor reels have come down in price this problem is easing.

2   Use plenty of backing (thick braided thread) on the reel drum before attaching line. This makes for freer flow and less turns of the reel when winding in line.

3   Light metal reels are more hard wearing than hard plastic which will crack with heavy use.

4   Select a reel which has a good range in 'drag' i.e. light to firm otherwise it can take an eternity to reel in.

5   Most mid range priced reels are technically well made these days though the more you pay the better they are, with the odd irritating exception.

6   Remember that if you clean and oil the reel's interior mechanisms frequently, it will last much longer.

7   If your line jams in the reel take the spool out and work on it separately. Trying to repair fankled lines within the drum is hopelessly time consuming.

8   Automatic rewind reels with a lever to pull in all your extended line quickly are very popular in European countries however they don't seem to have caught on in the UK. Actually they are quite useful once you get the hang of them but then fashion dictates!

Fly Lines

Terminology 'AFTM' refers to the weight of the line which should be used in conjunction with the rod. The AFTM line weighting is usually stamped on the rod just above the cork handle e.g. 4/5 or 6/7. 'DT' (double taper) lines are tapered either end and have a 'fatter' part in the middle. 'WF' (weight forward) lines have the bulk of the thicker heavier part of the line at the casting end, this assists casting across high winds and gives extra distance when used properly. 'Shooting Heads' are heavy WF lines which again potentially assist distance. Manufacturers' descriptions of what depth the line fishes in the water include 'floating', 'intermediate', 'sinking' or 'sink tip'. 'Fast' or 'Slow' sink refers to the speed the line goes down. The 'coating' refers to the outer synthetic coating on the line, manufacturers lay great emphasis on the coatings' smoothness (this helps casting) and its durability. 'Line friction' on the other hand is something to be avoided at all costs! Modern technology has also designed a variety of line extensions sometimes known as 'multi tips' which technically mean that you can alter depth without changing spools. If you do use these make sure they have a slick joining mechanism sometimes known as the hinge, otherwise these add ons can be absolute beasts to cast.

1   The line is the largest piece of equipment which comes into direct contact with the fish's environment, the rest of the Big Five do not even come close. Buy the best you can afford but beware of advertising claims that you can cut through gales, fish into the teeth of a wind etc. You may need specialist casting skills to achieve this if at all.

2   Always select a line with AFTM to balance the rod. Choosing a lighter line than the rod requires makes for very hard work on the casting arm. Using too heavy an AFTM puts excessive strain on the rod and increases its wear and tear.

3   Fly lines come in many shapes and sizes. Floating lines are the easiest by far to cast with, any line which sinks below the surface requires more effort to roll it up to the top before lifting off.

Buy the best fly line you can afford

4   If you are a complete beginner start learning with a DT floating line.

5   In general the cheaper the line the quicker it will crack and lose its aerialising qualities. Cheap lines also retain more memory and take forever to straighten out.

6   Replace your fly line every year if you use it frequently, every two years for less frequent usage.

7   When not in use, lines should be stored loosely off the reel (personally I often conveniently forget to do this as it is a bit of a hassle). Doing so however does extend the line's life considerably.

8   Remember that if you bank fish a lot many dirt particles are going to adhere themselves to the line. Cleaning it regularly makes casting much slicker.

9   Regular line maintenance i.e. cleaning and/or reconditioning extends its life no end no matter where you use it.

10   Be cautious of using separate sink tip attachments on your floating line. They often alter its casting qualities dramatically and can be difficult to operate successfully. An investment in a spare spool with a full length sink tip line might be a better option.

Nylon

Terminology Nylon is also known as a leader (see tapered and braided leader on page 47), tippet, fluorocarbon or, if you are of the older generation, the cast. BS is breaking strain of the nylon e.g. 5lbBS means the trout has to exert a pressure of quite a bit more than 5lb in order to break the nylon.

1   Choose a hard wearing nylon which turns over easily and stretches out quickly without kinks. For wild brown trout a breaking strain of 4lb is normally enough, sea trout may need 4lb to 8lbBS depending on the size of fish present.

2   Nylon which glitters in sunny conditions is a curse so choose nylon with as matt a finish as possible. Coloured nylon with a brown or greenish stain may be of some advantage though because of light properties in water of different depths the coloured tippets may not give quite the advantage you think.

3   Avoid very fine nylon of 3lbBS or less, if you are myopic it is difficult to see and it is also very difficult to work with in windy conditions. Maybe it is my age but I don't feel secure using less than 4lb nylon!

4   If you fish for trout with more than one fly you need nylon capable of supporting droppers. Nylon of less than 4lbBS tends to collapse and fold itself around the core of the leader. A slightly stiff nylon is better for this purpose.

5   When an angler is 'broken' by a fish it may not mean the fish exerted more than the BS he was using. Wind knots, poorly tied on flies and nylon which has become worn because it has not been changed recently account for many more 'breaks' than heavy fish!

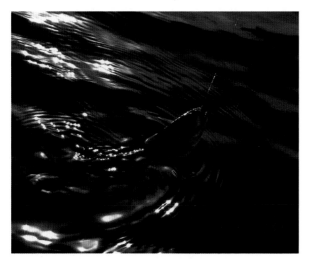

For wild brown trout nylon of 4lbBS is normally enough

6 Avoid ready made leaders with droppers already attached because they offer no flexibility in spacing out how the flies are to be attached.

7. Fluorocarbon has the same function as nylon, it is simply made of a different material. It is said to be more UV resistant (sunlight increases wear and tear on nylon), be less prone to abrasion and to hold brilliant knots. Most good nylons do the same so is it all manufacturers' hype?

41

Flies

Terminology Dry flies float, wet flies, lures and nymphs sink. Size 8 or 10 are about the largest flies used for wild trout, size 12 upwards to 18 gets correspondingly smaller. Hook, head, body, tail, wings, hackle, tying silk, rib, butt, tag, legs, thorax, abdomen, throat hackle are names of parts of the trout fly. For basic flies a hook, silk, body and hackle/wing are all that is needed. Barbless hooks are used when you want to return fish with the minimum damage.

TYPICAL TROUT FLY

1   Flies should be selected according to their main area of use (see also Chapter 10). Different trout fishing venues will usually demand different fly patterns (sparse, heavily dressed, hackled or with wings etc). Go for a cross section of patterns, but seek sound local advice first to avoid unnecessary flogging with patterns more suited to somewhere else.

2   For wild trout a fair range of standard wet, dry and nymph flies sizes 10 to 16 usually does the trick. Patterns will vary slightly according to whether they are intended for flowing or stillwater.

3   Over-the-counter bulk ready made selections of '12 Top Stream Fishers' or '24 Loch Specials' might sound good, but you will often find that half or more of the flies are not suited for their intended use.

4   Many flies sold in the UK and/or on the internet are made abroad, Kenya is a big supplier, and the quality of tying can vary considerably. Buy from a reputable supplier or better still make your own.

5   Beware flies which are gross adaptations (to the point of silliness) of a successful original. Soldier Palmers, for example, should not be dressed up in pink wool with shiny tinsel!

6   Store flies appropriately, for example dry flies with upright wings need extra space to keep their shape. Stuffing everything into one narrow box is not a good idea.

Go for a cross section of patterns

7   Keep dry flies and wets separate. If you use lots of floatant on dries it can 'infect' the wets if they are stored closed together. You will often find your sinking flies do all sorts of strange things!

These then are the Big Five; rod, reel, line, nylon, flies and they are essential for trout angling. Now let's look at the other bits and pieces.

ACCOUTREMENTS

The following accoutrements have been given an Indispensability Rating:
* = not much required up to ***** = as essential as the Big Five.

Fishing vest ***** This is a pretty mandatory piece of kit as, given enough pockets, you can carry with you all your flies, nylon, spare reel/spools, lunch, lightweight waterproof, gloves, midge net and so on. It can be worn inside the winter waterproof on cold days or once spring appears you can wear it out over a lightweight jerkin or fleece. Pick one suited to your size allowing for a jacket underneath otherwise your neck vertebrae can be uncomfortably pinched after wear. Ladies should note that so far few UK tackle suppliers have gone to the trouble of making

43

a well fitting fishing vest designed to fit a woman's shape although there are a couple made by different American companies which are good products.

Waterproofs **** A good light-weight jacket has as few seams as possible. Those seams which are there should be well taped and sealed for these are the joins in the material that leak first in heavy rain. If you walk a lot when fishing, investing in a breathable fabric should definitely be considered. I prefer light jackets made of material similar to Goretex, they are not so tiring to wear all day and you avoid getting too sweaty. Waxed cotton may be waterproof (if well treated) but it gets boiling hot in summer. Note that detachable jacket hoods on studs are not as useful as you think as the rain has a nasty habit of getting in at the join. Waterproof trousers are excellent for sitting in boats but ditto the heat/sweat factor if you have to walk far in them.

Accoutrements – a dram sometimes helps!

Flotation devices ***** Absolutely essential when deep wading and/or when going afloat. Cold water kills quickly (hypothermia) even if you consider your-self a strong swimmer. If you are of small build avoid a flotation device which is too cumbersome and heavy as it is exhausting wearing it all day. From experience I have found that the simple bar types which do not constrict your casting are more comfortable than a complete jacket style. Thankfully designs in flotation devices are improving and you need not resemble the trussed up chicken you once did.

Tackle bag **** For all day fishing a tackle bag for your accoutrements is essential. If however you are only fishing a few hours you can get by with your fishing vest (see above). When embarking on long walks to hill lochs or lots of shoreline angling I choose a lightweight rucksack with good padded back, interior pockets and shoulder straps. This allows me to walk and fish freely without having to take off the bag. Bags which fit only by a single shoulder strap are fine if you only need them to transport items from car to boat or down to the water's edge.

However if you walk miles with this type you can end up with shoulder ache for the bag's weight is not being distributed evenly. Also note that you should check the bag's construction as a well sealed waterproof base is essential particularly for boat angling where water sloshes up from under the duckboards and wets everything on the floor of the boat. Also the interior of the bag should have separate compartments for different items of gear and a detachable fish bass. If the bass is built in, it stinks after a while! At least two easily accessed exterior pockets are also essential so you do not have to keep opening the whole bag for smaller items.

Fleeces **** Fleece may be a comparatively new innovation in fishing gear but nowadays they are pretty commonplace. Basically they are the 'spare jersey' made in modern brushed cotton and/or synthetic materials. They have different 'tog ratings' for winter and summer use and have either half or full zips. I frequently use them in conjunction with a fishing vest and take a lightweight waterproof with me in case of rain. Fleeces are most effective when used as part of the layer system. Some come with a windproof lining which is excellent for winter wear but can be too hot in summer. They are much more pleasant to wear than scratchy wool unless of course you go in for cashmere.

Hats **** A fishing hat is perhaps more important than you think. Hats cut out glare saving you from burnt eyeballs, reduce the chances of a stray fly impaling itself in your nose and help keep the rain off on wet days. Peaked caps are best for this purpose, lightweight hats with wide brims blow off. Use a warm lined one with ear flaps for winter and a cotton hat for summer.

Waders **** Wading boots come in varieties according to wading depth i.e. thigh, waist or chest waders and are also classed by the type of sole on them. Thigh waders or at a pinch waist waders are recommended for waters where you must walk a lot. Chest waders can be used in either flowing or still water but follow local advice and go with caution. If you walk a considerable way wearing chest waders you are either very fit or very daft. Standard materials used in wader construction include

Studded sole waders are my recommendation for most situations

rubberised cotton (slightly cooler but still sweaty) and neoprene (warmer but not sweaty in balmy weather). Breathable fabrics which are lighter are more expensive but are definitely worth it if you intend doing a lot of wading.

Felt sole waders slip like mad on grass, peat and mud but grip quite well on slippery rocks. Felt sole with studs added will save you some embarrassment. Cleated soles grip reasonably well on grass and mud but often fail miserably to grip on algae-covered underwater rocks. Studded sole waders are my recommendation except in circumstances where the clinking of metal studs on the bottom is likely to spook fish, for example in small clearwater streams. Neoprene waders can be purchased with sock feet and these are then worn inside short boots (which for safety should have studs of some sort). If you buy these be sure of your sizing, you may find you cannot get the neoprene socks inside your normal shoe size! People with UK shoe sizes five or less will have trouble getting waders to fit, most are made in bigger sizes and lots of wool socks will be required to fill out the boots.

Wading stick ** to ***** Use common sense with a wading stick. If you are not as steady as you used to be and/or you are going to be wading deep fast water then one is essential. If on the other hand it will be bank fishing only or you are in a boat, wading sticks are obviously not really much required. I use my wading stick to help me over rough hill loch terrain especially going uphill when it is a boon, and it is also useful for testing the depth of bogs! However once I'm at the water I don't normally wade with it unless the water looks tricky with obvious drop offs.

Sunglasses *** Eyes are very important when fishing, treat them with care and kit yourself out with suitable UV protection. If you are myopic like me it might be prudent to invest in a pair of prescription shades – they are definitely worth it. Clip-ons are pretty useless in a big wind, they either flip up unexpectedly or worse still blow off. I committed several to the drink before moving up to prescription sunglasses. Any spectacles will protect eyes from stray flies (shades or not) so don't be without them.

Scissors and snips *** My dentist does not recommend using teeth to bite nylon and I doubt yours would either. Scissors are more cumbersome in cold weather when your hands are numb but can have the important little addition of forceps on the end to extract flies from deep in the throat of a trout. Snips are much quicker but are not much use for such extractions. They are best attached to your person by way of a retractable zinger.

Midge repellent/midge nets * to *** Necessity of this piece of kit depends very much on where you are fishing. Biting midges are at their most prevalent in the Scottish Highlands during July and August. They favour a peat, heather and bog environment though conifers also harbour plenty of the little black pests. Hatching conditions are still and overcast with or without drizzle. In a fierce attack no repellent or head net is truly effective but you can lessen the agony by being prepared before you go. Coating yourself in midge repellent prior to fishing and putting on the net immediately the first midge emerges sometimes works. They are not necessary throughout the UK however as many southern areas are midge free (lucky them!).

Nets *** In England it is now the law that you must use a knotless net i.e. the material mesh must not be knotted together as this can damage the scales and flanks of the fish before you are able to return it. Knotless nets are fish friendly and are therefore highly recommended for use throughout the UK. For boat fishing you normally need one with an extending handle as you may have to net the fish at some distance. For bank fishing a short handled net normally is sufficient. Make sure you attach it to your person with either extendable elastic or a quick release mechanism – it is the devil's own job to detach it otherwise when struggling with a fighting trout. Nets are advised when boat angling, float tubing, wading at a significant distance from the shore or fishing from a very high bank. Otherwise you can beach the trout (I only beach fish if I intend to keep them for dinner) or, if using barbless hooks, bring it to hand and shake it off back into the water with minimum scale damage.

Floatant and sink *** These are small bottles or sprays of slightly greasy goo or clear liquid which either assist flies in floating up top or makes them disappear toward the bottom. They are useful if you fish a lot of different depths. Remember floatant has to be reapplied if a trout takes hard and musses up the dry flies hackles.

Tapered and/or braided leaders ** to *** These are used to attach fly to fly line and come in various lengths (5ft to 9ft are the most common). With tapered leaders the concept is not a new one, in fact it goes right back to horsehair 'casts' which were woven down to a single hair on to which the fly was attached. Today the tapered leader is graduated from thicker nylon at the fly line end to fine thin nylon at the tippet where the fly is to be tied on. Advantages are a good turnover but disadvantages are inflexibility in leader length and you cannot attach droppers; also if you change your fly a lot, you quickly run out of the very fine tip. Braided leaders are add ons to the fly line, most makes feature some tapering but to use them you must attach a piece of nylon at the end to tie on your fly. They are made of very soft supple material and are said to reduce line memory and provide a smoother lift off of the fly line. Braided leaders can be fished at different depths i.e. floating to fast sink, so select one suitable to your local water. Neither of these leaders are absolutely essential pieces of kit but they might just up the catch rate a little, I have used both and not found much difference so I reserve judgement.

Drogues **** Purely for use with the boat, these large cotton or canvas bags fold out and hang behind the boat to slow down the drift. They are exceptionally useful on big exposed waters when the drift is lengthy, but a bit of a nuisance when the drifts are short as they have to be hauled up out of the way for the return journey.

Boat fishing requires comfort extras like cushions and drogues

Plastic cushion **** Again for the boat; whilst it might look a bit sissy carting it down to the craft you will be the one with a happy posterior at the end of a long day afloat.

Sight indicators * Strictly non purist they come in luminescent coloured blobs and you stick them about 5ft from the point fly. If the bob or indicator suddenly jerks you might have a trout. Might be good if you are partially sighted but is this not what they call float fishing?

Other bits * to **** My tackle bag/rucksack also contains a whistle, OS map, a compass, bottle of water, some food and emergency sugar sweets and a light fold-out space blanket (a thin wrap that looks like tin foil). If you are fishing all day in a remote wilderness area these are vital especially if you are benighted, lose your way and/or the mist comes down. However if you are only going to a stocked pond just around the corner they might not be deemed so essential!

TROUTFISHER'S TOP TIPS FOR CHOOSING TACKLE

1   Go with what feels physically comfortable to you, advertising hype is all very well but anglers are diverse characters with different physiques and abilities.

2   Choose kit suitable to where you will most use it.

3   Remember the Big Five and start with them, everything else is secondary.

4
TO CAST A FLY

'A merry duffer is better than a dour master'
Roderick Haig Brown

Colleague, friend and well regarded 'Oracle' Geoffrey Bucknall once said to me that most fly casting techniques are actually very easy, it is just that to outsiders they can seem elaborately difficult and novices can feel such skills are unattainable. Most of us who have been fishing a long time are very comfortable in handling rods and can make things look pretty effortless. However place your rod in the hands of a beginner with all that line, nylon and flies to control and blind panic is often the result. Non familiarity is a daunting thing when taking up a new sport. Take heart though for even the most cack-handed amongst us can make perfunctory casts with a little helpful guidance. Learning to cast is like learning any other sporting technique, get a good teacher and then allow time to practise on your own, Rome was never built in one proverbial day.

Casting is all about presentation

Before you start I ask you to do two things. The first is to place a fly in your palm and feel the weight of this tiny object you are about to propel on to water. A trout fly is a dainty, elegant piece of silk and feather and your casting effort should match its delicateness. We are not talking sledgehammers to crack nuts here. The second thing I would like you to do is fix in your mind that you are casting a fly to catch a fish not to show mastery of the aerialised line. Macho distance casting which appears to take an inordinate amount of muscle (it doesn't really, the secret is in the timing) is not what we are about here. Casting is not about show, the trout don't care two hoots whether you can cast fifteen yards or fifty. It is all about presentation, putting your fly over fish without scaring them and then trying to stimulate a response. Somehow in this modern age, casting and presentation are sometimes looked upon as two different skills. Casting is for hurtling line into infinity whereas presentation is fishing to a definite rise. Nonsense. Every time you cast you present your fly to a trout which might seize your offering.

ASSEMBLING YOUR GEAR

If you have done all this before you can skip this part. Rod and reel assembly is comparatively easy after all and I shall not dwell too much on it. Here are a few quick hints to save time and temper.

1   Press home the ferrules gently but firmly otherwise the rod sometimes flies apart with over enthusiastic casting.

2   Make sure the guides/rings are aligned and that as you thread the line through, you do not miss any of them out.

3   Remember to put the reel on according to whether you are right handed or left handed. To accommodate these differences some reels allow you to reverse the wind-in action.

4   It is usual to have the winder on the reel facing into the body so as to reel in with your free hand however some of us face the winder out and change hands to reel in! Use what is most comfortable for your purposes.

5   There are various knots to join nylon to fly line, I use a loop to loop system but whatever knot you use remember to flatten and tighten it, a little bit of spit helps it all stick together. Unsecured knots will tend to slip usually when you have the fish of a lifetime attached.

6   Do not store nylon on the reel. It buries itself between the fly line and this can be incredibly annoying when trout are rising and you want to get at them quickly.

7   Clean gear periodically but not obsessively, just enough to keep it in good working order.

8   When you have finished fishing take down rod and line and store in their containers. It is supposed to prolong the life of equipment but I must admit that tiredness doesn't always make me do it!

KEY ELEMENTS OF CASTING

The Overhead cast is probably where most of us begin our fishing careers however the Roll and the Snake Roll are also covered as they can be extremely useful for presenting a fly in difficult circumstances. In learning any of these techniques there is no substitute for expert hands-on instruction. Though I can describe casting actions, you will learn a lot quicker if a qualified instructor or at least an experienced knowledgeable angler is at your elbow.

THE OVERHEAD CAST

This cast can be used on stillwater or flowing, from the bank or the boat and is the most commonly used in the UK. Follow the key elements listed below, remembering to keep your body balanced and staying within your 'casting space'. As with a swing plane in golf there is a definite 'casting plane' involved in the Overhead cast. Sometimes you will see this referred to as a tight loop or even a sexy one! You will know when you do not stay within this casting plane as it all goes pear shaped with the line either snagged behind or deposited in a crumpled heap. Keep your tempo light and relaxed.

The basic fundamentals are always the same for the Overhead cast.

... **Start low...lift...pause...throw**. Note the use of the word 'throw'. This is sometimes frowned upon in some teaching circles as the casting action is not really like throwing a ball, though I personally feel it does bear a vague resemblance to throwing a dart. However since many of the late and great used the term 'throw' for example Bowlker in the 1700s '*When you see a fish rise, the best way is to throw a yard above him*', I have no problem in using it now. The Overhead is a universally accepted cast with lots of advantages in terms of distance and accuracy. The only time you may have difficulty executing it is when your casting is obstructed in some way perhaps with high banks or trees directly behind. The timing of the components of the cast i.e. the coordination of the backcast and the forward throw can also be awkward to get right in difficult winds and frustration can be the end result. Persevere however for there is much to commend this cast.

Key Elements of Overhead Casting

- If you are a complete novice at casting, choose a day with a light wind either behind or slightly to one side. Don't begin in a screaming gale if you can help it.

51

- Before you start make sure your body is balanced, straighten your back and have both arms lightly crooked at the elbow. Relax your free hand at your side loosely holding the line.

- With the rod tip parallel to the water pull or shake out enough line (two rod lengths is fine) on to the water. Begin the cast with the rod tip low and lift off line from there. This uses all the casting plane to generate a crisp cast. If you start with the rod pointing skyward you will struggle to generate distance.

- Use the rod like a lever to lift the line off the water with a progressive acceleration. Speed is not important, a smooth rhythm is required. Bring the rod butt to the perpendicular toward the side of your head with a clean easy movement.

Keep your body balanced and relaxed

- To keep the line airborne (sometimes termed loading the rod) use the water surface to generate smooth acceleration which gets the line moving fast and generates enough speed to get the line up and into the air. A slight flick at the top of the Overhead and Snake cast will propel the line out behind and stretch it out in a loop. Once the rod is perpendicular rod and wrist will be somewhere near head height with the butt of the rod pointing towards the ground. The wrist is not 'broken' i.e. bent back past the upright position as this takes the 'ping' out of the cast and alters its momentum.

- To project the line and fly forward use a tap or a flick rather like flicking a lump of mud off the end of the rod. Note the power of this tap may have to be varied according to the wind speed and direction but it is not normally a brutal movement. Trying to push forward too hard actually takes the line out of the casting plane/arc and a messy end result usually follows.

- Despite what you might see in casting competitions, once the line is in the air you do not need to turn your head round/up to look at it curl and uncurl. The trout are in the water not the clouds.

Use the water surface to generate line speed and smoothly lift off for the Overhead cast

- Once you are engaged in the forward throw for the Overhead and the Snake cast (which has the same finish) the line should travel at similar speed to the lift off. Aim high at the horizon and then as you release the line, gravity will gently take it down on to the water surface. Once there the rod arm is gently returned to the crooked elbow position to begin the retrieve.

Aim high on the forward throw

- Some instructors will teach Overhead casting by the clock face which is a standard established method. My personal preference is not to do this as I believe casting is about balance and feel. You are trying to propel a fly to catch a fish, not to follow the numbers of a clock. However, if you have a more clinical numerical bent you may find this helpful.

THE ROLL CAST

When you Roll cast the fly line does not travel up and behind in its familiar over-head plane and instead you keep it all relatively close to the body. This makes a Roll cast ideal for tight corners where high banks or overhanging undergrowth restrict your technique. It is is also a useful ploy when fishing lengthy days from the boat as it is not so tiring especially in high winds. Casting long lines are not normally necessary when afloat and Roll casting allows you to fish comfortably all day without too much effort. Note that sometimes (though not always!) beginners find a Roll cast easier to execute than the Overhead and it is worthwhile bearing this in mind if you are having trouble mastering the Overhead cast.

Key Elements of Roll Casting

- To execute the 'roll' keep the rod tip parallel to the water and shake out enough line (at least two rod lengths) on to the water and point the rod tip at the fly.

- Draw the rod tip round to your left or right side keeping it more or less parallel to the water. Though technically you can execute Roll casts over either shoulder it is more comfortable to use the left side for left handers and the right for right handers.

- With the rod parallel to the bank draw the rod smoothly up towards head height. A large loop or belly will appear in the line which has now drawn nearer to the rod. It looks like a capital D.

In Roll casting draw the rod smoothly to the side and then up to the head. This creates a capital D between line and rod

- Once the rod is perpendicular you can give it a forward tap in a downward action. This is the only cast when you deliberately tap down towards the water surface rather than higher at the horizon. The tap has the effect of turning the line over in a complete roll and with practise the fly will be returned to the water with minimum effort.

- With a Roll cast the action is a slow acceleration using the surface tension of the water to build up speed.

- The secret of success in Roll casting is to keep the whole action fluid. There is no pause between lift off and forward throw as there is with the Overhead cast.

- The only disadvantage with using Roll casting is that there can be quite a bit of water disturbance as you are building up line speed and also your length of cast cannot be adjusted easily.

- Remember it is essential to use a Roll cast to draw up a sinking or intermediate line to the surface before aerilising it again and if you use sunk lines a lot it is essential to learn the Roll cast. For floating line fishing its principal use is to avoid entanglements on the back cast.

Success in Roll casting comes from keeping the action continuous and fluid

THE SNAKE ROLL CAST

This cast is extremely useful when fishing a floating line and dry fly. It enables you to pick virtually all the line off the water in one go and redirect it without the lengthy process of retrieving it all back before recasting. At a pinch it can also be used with a team of wet flies providing they are on a high floating line. This makes it an exceptionally useful weapon when trout are rising enthusiastically in different spots and you need to change direction quickly to cover them.

Key Elements of the Snake Roll

- The principal difference between this cast and the Overhead is the way the line is lifted off the water and brought into play.

- Instead of using the standard overhead lift off, leave the line extended in front of you and draw the rod tip round in two brisk circles toward your body i.e. anti clockwise if right handed, clockwise for the left handed.

- This creates a 'Snake Roll' in the line and once you see these circles appearing lift off quickly up to the high Overhead casting plane and then continue into the normal overhead cast to redirect your fly where you have seen the trout rise.

- With the Snake Roll the action has to be quite brisk to get the line airborne. If you are too gentle nothing much happens. It can take a little while to get the timing right but it is a very useful skill to have in your armoury especially when a number of trout are feeding greedily in front of you.

- The only disadvantage I can see is the small splash the line makes when you circle it around. This does not make the Snake Roll the ideal choice for crystal clear waters where trout are easily spooked, but if there is a ripple it is easily enough disguised.

- The Snake Roll is probably best learnt once you are proficient with the Overhead and the Roll cast but once learnt you will find yourself at a considerable advantage and with practise you can Snake Roll your line into the air and then false cast to lengthen or shorten line according to where the target (the trout) is rising.

With the Snake Roll cast lift off smartly into the Overhead casting plane

CASTING PROPELS YOUR FLY – NOW COMES THE RETRIEVE

Whatever casting technique you use there is still a need to retrieve the line back to the starting point. The retrieve is a vital part of casting yet it is sometimes ignored by expert casters who favour technique in distance. Casting fifty yards might look good but ask yourself the serious question is there a trout there anyway? Retrieving the fly is the part of the cast that the trout are most likely to notice, they really are not interested in the fact the fly apparently flew out half a mile to reach them.

Key Elements of the Retrieve

- It is essential that once the fly is in the water you must give it a life-like appearance.

- Remember that trout recognise their prey first by the way it moves. Thus a shiny lure-like fly such as the Dunkeld which at a pinch imitates a small struggling fish, should be worked with a retrieve which makes it lift and dart like the real thing. Equally a dry fly like a Sedge imitation may scuttle on the surface and your retrieve must reflect this movement.

- At all times your retrieve must be made passing behind the middle index finger of your rod hand so that should a fish take, you can simply clamp the line to the rod with your rod hand and lift into it.

- With your free hand retrieve your line back towards you at a suitable pace. The excess will fall loosely at your feet. Though you might be tempted to use a line tray which gathers the line together in front of you, these things are hugely cumbersome and make your casting technique awkward. I never recommend them.

- Keep your balance and do not pull out huge lengths of line away to one side of your body. This might work for rainbow trout but with your free hand stretched so far out of your casting plane when a wild trout does take you will often miss it completely.

- As a general rule wet fly is retrieved at a medium to fast pace, dry fly

Retrieve the line through the middle index finger

57

can be fished semi static or with a slow twitch retrieve while nymphs are normally fished with a slow retrieve.

- A slight lifting and lowering of the rod tip will cause your imitation to rise and fall in the water and can add extra life to the fly. This is useful for nymph fishing and also when 'twitching' a dry fly.

- When you want to retrieve slowly instead of a 'figure of eight' retrieve which bunches up the line in your hand sometimes creating excess memory especially in a cheap fly line, use the same style pace of slow retrieve under the index finger of the rod hand but let the line fall loosely below you. Personally I find all that scrunched up line in your free hand distracting and I have had beginners turn round in a panic when they hook a fish saying 'What do I do with all this line?' Do a figure of eight by all means but let it go. Alternatively you can use lovely 'fingering' or 'hand twist' method. This is an old but quite effective method I found described in Colonel Oatts' book *Loch Trout* written in the 1950s. It is not used so much nowadays as the rod index finger is not used to trap line when a fish takes and this can lead to a loss of control over the proceedings.

LENGTHENING/SHOOTING LINE

Most anglers want to lengthen the distance they cast but it must be emphasised that huge distances are not normally what wild trout fishing is about. Casting into infinity may look great but more often than not a) you will have lined and spooked at least half a dozen trout doing so and b) it is almost impossible to set the hook in anything that far away! However sometimes trout persist in rising off the far bank or just on the ripple outwith your usual range. Here is some advice on 'going further'.

Key Elements of Lengthening Line

- To enable you to 'lengthen' your cast you need to generate more line speed. You begin this action by pulling off a bit of extra line from the reel while you are still fishing out your retrieve. Go canny at first as over ambitious ideas on how much line you are going to cast results in a splashy nightmare guaranteed to spook trout.

- Finish your retrieve say 8 to10 yards away.

- Now reach forward to the first rod ring and pull down on the line at the same time as you lift off to cast again.

- With this action you use the surface tension of the water to increase line speed quite considerably and this should allow you to'shoot' out that extra line you have lying at your feet. Shooting line simply means propelling line forward while keeping control of it with your free hand.

THE STRIKE

Striking a trout is not that difficult. You need only lift the rod crisply as if you are going to cast again and you will set the hook. Unfortunately where we can go wrong in this is in the timing of the actual connection between rod, line and fish. Some wild trout take languidly and it is easy to rush setting the hook and only end up pulling the fly away from the fish's mouth. On the other hand some fish will make a lightning fast rise at the fly and will be on and off again before you have done anything at all. It has even been known for browns to leap skyward with the fly in their jaws and if you do not set the hook while they are airborne they will have rejected your offering by the time they re-enter the water! – To lessen the times you are left aghast at the missed opportunity let's look at essentials in striking the fish.

Key Elements of Striking Trout

- It is essential to have the line trapped under the index finger of your rod hand, when you feel a pluck or pull clamp line to rod and lift immediately as if casting again.

- Timing is critical but while your strike should be firm enough to set the hook it should not be so brutal that it breaks the fish's jaw.

- Once contact with the trout is made keep the rod high and in the perpendicular, pulling it to one side often pulls the fly out of the fish's mouth.

- Play the trout gently but with control, do not prolong the fight unnecessarily.

Strike firmly but not brutally, then keep the rod in the perpendicular until the fish is ready for the net

FALSE CASTING

I am not a fan of excessive false casting. It might look skilfully macho but unless there is a drastic need for it, a simple one or two false casts in order to make the fly line fish at a longer distance from the shore are enough for me. Trout cannot be caught while the fly whirls and birls around your ears, they can only be taken while your offering is in actual contact with the water. The more times you flash the line back and forth above the water the more you increase the chances of spooking the trout.

I prefer to call a false cast a method of lengthening line as the insertion of a false cast when the line is in the air does allow you to cover more distance without overly disturbing the water surface. Accuracy is however more important than distance for its own sake. If you are fishing one way and see a trout rise at a different spot, point the rod tip at the rings of the rise and then lift your fly line off the water to recast. Do this in a smooth continuous motion rather than pointing the rod at the fish and pausing. Point and lift off for maximum effect. Then, by keeping the line in the air for one or two false casts, you should technically be able to alter line length and direction quickly and cover that trout.

MENDING LINE

This is one of those tricks which can be made to sound very difficult but is really quite simple to execute. In stillwater fishing where you have cast your line across a brisk wind you may well want to mend line so as to keep the fly more or less straight in front as you retrieve. To mend successfully the line once your fly has alighted give a light but positive semi circular roll of the rod tip upwind. This should help straighten out the rapidly appearing belly in the line and keep you in better contact with the fly.

Similarly in stream fishing the current will have a distorting effect on your cast. If you do not mend the line upstream quickly, the fly line will often belly out ahead of your fly. If you are not careful all the trout sees is a mass of fly line bearing down on him rather than your carefully cast fly which is trailing along somewhere behind. Again a semi circular roll of the rod tip upstream should push the offending belly back a little.

SOME COMMON CASTING PROBLEMS AND SOLUTIONS

The line comes down with a hefty splash You are using too much brute force and/or not allowing the rod time to flex as the propelling lever. Lift the line off smoothly, pause and then aim the fly out toward the horizon **above** the water and let it drift down gently. Keep your back straight and your casting arm gently hinged at the finish rather than straight. Pointing the rod out over the water at the end of the cast interrupts its momentum.

The fly keeps getting caught behind on the bank The line trajectory is too low. When lifting off line bring the rod up to the perpendicular a bit closer to your head to maximise height. Don't bend your wrist back on the backcast as this action brings the line closer to the ground behind you. Also resist pointing the rod tip sideways to cast as this automatically makes the trajectory lower. Stay within your own casting plane and pause between lift and throw.

Keep your back straight, aim your forward cast high toward the horizon and let line and fly drift down gently

The wind makes a mess of my cast If the wind is from behind and blowing the line down, lift your casting arm a little higher. If you are wanting to cast across the wind, try turning side on and putting your shoulder or back into the wind. Also learn to cast over both the left and the right shoulder or you will be scuppered in a Highland gale!

My back is aching after half an hour of casting You are trying to impel force with your body rather than using synchronised arm and rod action. Resist the temptation to lean forward at the end of a cast. Stand tall and let the rod do its work.

My wrist and/or arm are stiff and sore after a short period More than likely you are gripping the rod too hard and/or 'breaking' the wrist in a vain effort to get extra momentum. Remember you are casting an object of incredible flimsiness. Relax your hands, arms and shoulders so the rod is held with a light, easy grip. Keep the rod under your wrist as if it is an extension of your arm when you cast, tuck the butt in your jersey sleeve if you need a reminder to keep control.

I'm not getting much distance despite mighty efforts You are probably rushing the cast and not allowing enough time for the rod to work as a lever in aerilising and releasing the line. Also the timing of shooting line i.e. running it through your fingers may be out. Use your free hand as the control. Rather than thinking solely distance give yourself a target to aim at, preferably a rising fish.

My casting feels awkward with my body scrunched up This often happens if you keep following the movement of the rod with your free hand. Try and avoid crossing your body with your other arm. Keep your stance open and fluid.

TROUTFISHER'S TOP TIPS ON CASTING

1   Casting is a waltz not a tango.

2   Presenting a fly gently and with grace is what we all aspire to, the rod and line should work in sweet harmony which does come with practise.

3   Before casting balance your body, think relaxed symmetry not strained chaos.

4   If it hurts you are not doing it correctly.

5   Remember casting is a necessary fifty per cent of fishing but the rest is water-craft and that is just as important.

5

GENERAL GUIDE TO TROUT FISHING TECHNIQUES

'Good judgement comes from experience, and experience – well that comes from poor judgement'
Anon

A WORD ON FLEXIBLE FISHING

Once you have gained a degree of proficiency in the basics of casting you will want to advance your skills by practising the different techniques involved. Basically these fall into three categories; wet fly, dry fly and nymph fishing. In each case you are presenting a fly in a particular way to a trout which is either visible or you think might be lying in a certain position at a certain depth. Though as a general rule each skill will be common to a particular venue, for example wet fly fishing is often used on lochs and reservoirs while dry fly may be used more on clear limestone rivers, it is vital to remember that you can use all three fishing skills anywhere. Nothing in trout fishing is written in tablets of stone. Be flexible rather than entrenched. Adapting and moving seamlessly between different techniques according to what the conditions dictate should be everyone's goal.

Trout are amongst the most versatile of creatures and we must follow their example. Fish have no pretensions about method and do not give two hoots whether you send them an upstream dry or a well sunk wet. What does matter is that the fly you present to the trout must arouse curiosity rather than fear and/or that the pattern generally fits in with the feeding response happening at that time. For this reason you must take a little time out to assess the conditions, the likely natural feeding and how best to conceal your intentions both before and during your fishing day. If you want consistent success staying stuck in one particular technical groove despite obviously altering fishing factors is not going to achieve much. Entrenched fishing is less productive and frequently boring!

WET FLY BASICS

A basic definition of wet fly angling (also known as 'traditional', 'sunk fly' or 'loch style') might be to fish a submerged rather than floating fly below the surface of the water. This historic technique can be used confidently on either flowing or still water. The main objective of wet fly angling is to catch fish at the depth they are feeding. The trouble is that trout rarely lay up at one particular depth all the time. In stillwaters the feeding margins dry out as summer progresses, in rivers the force and depth of flow fluctuates according to the amount of rain and/or snow melt. Thus changes in water depth, temperature and water quality as well as the varying degree of safe cover from predators mean that trout have to be flexible in their choice of habitat at any given time during the season. We must therefore be equally adaptable and use an assortment of ruses to find the right depth at which to sink our flies…

RIVER WET FLY TECHNIQUE

- For sunk fly stream angling you can use anything from a single wet to perhaps three differing patterns. The old masters used a 'strap' of flies, up to twelve at one go, and despite little or no admission in their books, there must have been some horrific tangles! Nowadays modern anglers will normally use one, two or at a push three flies.

- The fly at the end of the nylon is the point fly and the other flies are known as droppers. Droppers should be well spaced apart (preferably 5ft to 6ft) and usually they should look unrelated.

- The object of all wet fly angling is to deceive a trout into thinking that what is drifting downstream on an underwater current is either an edible feast or an invader which he should attack and deal with in smart fashion.

- You can fish wet fly on a floating, intermediate or sinking line. Choose fly lines according to the speed of flow as much as according to river depth. Too light a (floating) line in spates means the fly is whisked round at such a speed it takes a trout of Schumacher mentality to want to chase it. Too heavy a line for the local depth of water means you stick on the bottom and/or the fly does not travel as it should.

- In the stream the current is master of the wet fly, it gives the fly life and you must follow its lead. Mend the line upstream if it is appearing to travel down stream ahead of the fly. You want a natural presentation of your pattern as if the line has nothing whatsoever to do with it.

- Normally you fish wet fly by casting across the stream and allowing the flow to swing the fly downstream in a gentle natural-looking arc. This technique is not written in a tablet of stone however and sometimes upstream wet fly is used, especially in tight situations with obstructions.

- Single wet fly is best when the local fishing habitat is difficult with lots of underwater rocks, weed or similar obstructions. The dropper fly will often snag especially if your catch is a spirited one.

- If you prefer, you can add a specially weighted braided leader on to the end

In the stream the current is master of the wet fly

of your floating line. This will allow you to alter the depth at which your fly swims.

- If you do not favour the braided leader approach you can stick a heavy fly such as a tungsten nymph at the point. This has the effect of drawing the dropper fly down quickly to mid depth.

- An old Indian trick in high fast water is to put a hefty tungsten nymph on a dropper about 3ft above your traditional wet fly. This sinks rapidly and acts almost as an 'anchor' to your normal pattern. This may sound daft but I have seen it catch trout when conditions looked utterly hopeless!

- Avoid showing too much of yourself to the fish. As you are casting and walking down pause for a moment to see what is behind you. If you are throwing a big shadow or standing tall like a telegraph pole on the bank, take a step back from the water's edge and lower your profile.

STILLWATER WET FLY TECHNIQUE

- Other terminology for stillwater wet fly method can include 'traditional wet' or 'loch style' but it is basically all a similar business with wet flies being fished in a life-like fashion below the water surface.

- For wet/sunk fly stillwater fishing you can use anything from one to four flies on one length of nylon. The point fly is the one at the sharp end and all the rest are attached as droppers.

- Leaders are at least the same length as your rod if not longer and your droppers should be spaced at least 4ft apart and preferably 6ft. Droppers which are too close together can be a threat to a trout especially if you make a hash of the cast and they all come crashing down at once.

- Traditional and loch style wet fly usually demands a floating line, more modern stillwater wet fly technique can mean fishing wet fly on a range of floating, intermediate and sinking lines.

- As there is no current as such (though the wind will play a goodly part) you must use differently paced retrieves to give your fly some credibility. In general terms wet fly can be retrieved at medium, fast or slow pace with medium being the most commonly used retrieve.

- The fundamental technique is to cast out your fly out and then retrieve it back to about a rod's length away before lifting off and casting again to a slightly different spot. Casting slightly across the wind rather than with the wind directly behind will aid your fly presentation.

- Casting should be methodical rather than random and you should always aim for likely trout holding areas such as edges of weed beds, by boulders, near ledges and so on.

Fish down the bank as fast as the drifting boat

- Keep moving as you fish, you want to cover new water all the time. Fish down the bank as fast as you would in the drifting boat.

- When fishing wet fly from the boat the basics are the same as when fishing off the bank. Work the fly or flies around likely trout holding spots (normally nearer the margins where feeding is more profuse). If you are using droppers (and from a boat this is definitely advisable), then just before you recast lift the rod tip to dibble the top dropper on the surface. The splashy, struggling movement of the fly often attracts trout and they will make a violent snatch at it.

- A single wet fly is effective on stillwaters especially from the bank when conditions such as flat calms are causing grief and consternation. Some loch style aficionados will scoff at this idea claiming you must have a minimum of two flies but it works for me!

- If you feel depth is required use either a weighted fly or a 'wee double' (a size 10 or 12 trout fly with two hooks) on the point fly. Nowadays you can even acquire some heavy malleable goo which you can carefully apply to the head of your fly to make it sink deeper – clever stuff but it is a little difficult to remove once applied. If you convert traditional wet flies with this weighted putty it really has got to be left on them.

DRY FLY BASICS

A basic definition of dry fly angling (also sometimes known as 'upstreaming', 'floating fly' or 'static fly') might be to fish your fly with it sitting on top of the water surface rather than sunk below it. Dry fly can be used quite happily on either flowing or stillwater. As we have seen already, considerable elitist mystique has surrounded the use of dry fly on rivers, mainly stemming from obsessive followers of Halford. However dry fly is an exciting, exacting technique to use anywhere. It is thrilling to cast to a rise, see the trout believe your artificial is real and take it down with gusto. It still constantly amazes me that when there is a dense hatch of mayfly the trout will take a well ginked artificial Green Drake against the natural ones all around it. I can only put this is down to pure greed, the artificial must look like a meatier version of the real thing. Whatever the reason this is real fishing in its purest form. However just because I and many like me love dry fly fishing this does not elevate it into the realms of daft 'Dray Flay' snobbery which at one time threatened to submerge the simple pleasures of our sport.

The main objective when using dry fly is to fool a trout into thinking your fly is a natural one which has just magically alighted on the water in front of his nose. While there is nothing to stop you casting a dry fly in random fashion, it is much more rewarding to cast towards a feeding fish. This is true sight fishing or stalking of trout (see also Chapter 7) and it always has an extra degree of excitement about it.

It is often said that dry fly catches the bigger resident trout. I'm not one hundred per cent sure about this but I do know dry fly is particularly useful in stillwaters for bringing otherwise dour trout suddenly and dramatically up to the surface. Also in rivers, a small dry will often winkle out sneaky larger trout which have tucked themselves into far bank hidey holes.

A small dry fly will often attract the larger trout

RIVER DRY FLY TECHNIQUE

Principal techniques for dry fly on flowing water include the following:

- Cast your dry fly upstream or slightly to one side ahead of a rising trout and let it drift down naturally without 'drag' i.e. a drift which is too fast to imitate a natural insect. While putting line and fly ahead of the waiting trout is accepted as the principal method for dry fly, I often cast up and across rather than straight upstream. It is sometimes difficult to control the line in a fast flow if it returns straight back toward you. Also if the trajectory is not exactly right, 'lining' the fish is often the unwanted result.

- In the end wind direction will always dictate the choice of line trajectory, sometimes your only choice will be across and down or even more or less straight downstream. This may not give the best presentation but as long as you keep yourself clear of the trout's view, it is worth a try.

- Once your fly is on the water it is important to keep control of the line as much as possible. You have to mend line upstream and fish with raised rod tip to keep the bulk of the line off the water so it does not present itself to the trout before the fly.

- After casting, follow the fly down by keeping the raised rod tip in line with it and if a trout takes all that is needed is a fast but smooth lift/strike to secure the hook.

- Upstream dry fly is quite hard work on the arms, you must frequently cast and lift off again before the fly swings too far round on the 'dangle'.

- Spotting rising trout is critical but even if nothing is showing remember the trout holding spots mentioned in Chapter 7. Go for shaded parts of pools, under overhanging branches, at the head or the tail of a pool, behind rocks which create eddies and so on.

- River trout like to keep station where food is funnelled down on the current to them and also where they can easily access shelter. Aim your dry fly ahead of their holds and let it drift in on the current.

- Select your pattern according to the size and general colour of what is hatching, absolutely exact imitations are not always necessary. This is not always as easy as it sounds, for though there may be a major hatch of say large olives going on, the trout may actually be gulping down a mouthful as small as a reed smut!

- Anoint your fly with suitable floatant before commencing battle and then again after each fish is caught.

River trout like to keep station where food is going to be channelled down to them   69

- Use a false cast to realign your fly direction but do not get obsessed with it. In the past false casting became closely linked to dry fly angling because you used it to dry out the fly. Similarly trapping air in the hackles by false casting used to be necessary in pre floatant days, nowadays chemicals have similar if not better effects.

- If you can cast lightly across or slightly upstream on to grassy vegetation (not trees!) and then gently tug it off so that the fly falls naturally into the water you can give the fly an ultra lifelike appearance almost guaranteed to attract a trout if there is one nestled below the bank.

- Use non glitter nylon of 3lb or 4lb and keep your flies fairly sparse and smaller than for the loch (size 14 to 22 are used though I personally cannot see well enough to thread a size 22!).

- Keep your profile merged into the bank and as much out of the fish's eye line as possible.

STILLWATER DRY FLY TACTICS

- Dry fly in stillwaters is particularly effective during major surface hatches when trout are up and feeding enthusiastically. However you can also use dry fly when the water is relatively calm and also in dour conditions when the wets are being ignored. Dry fly will work from as early as April right through to September when the conditions are right.

- Choose your dry fly roughly according to what size of insect is being hit by the trout. Size is often more important than colour when fishing dry fly. When mayfly or large olives are being taken put on a similar sized artificial.

- There is of course no current to make your dry fly move in a life-like way in stillwater, however do not be deterred from using the wind to your advantage or, if there is no breeze, simply fish a static dry in different spots around the lake/loch.

- Dry flies can be fished singly in light winds or in pairs in a good blow. Personally I do not use more than two dry flies on a stillwater cast and am careful to space the droppers out well (6ft apart). I have found anything closer together will sometimes spook trout rather than attract them.

- A dry fly top dropper with a wet fly on the point is a deadly combination providing the flies are well spaced so as to look unrelated and to fish them at different depths. Halford might spin in his grave but if it attracts trout I should get on with it!

- In general the retrieve should be slower than for wet fly. Often if trout are taking freely on the surface you may not need to retrieve at all for the dry fly will be snatched as soon as it hits the surface. If not, retrieve gently then twitch the rod tip up a shade to make the fly stutter on the surface in a lifelike way.

Choose your stillwater dry fly according to the size of local hatching natural insects

- Rises to dry fly in stillwaters vary from an almighty splash to a gentle roll over. Usually you have to pause slightly before setting the hook so that the fish has enough time to turn down on the fly. The only exception to this is the 'Aerial Route' rise when the fish is leaping skywards with the fly already in its jaws. Speed is then of the essence when striking.

- Keep the fly well greased so that it sits high in the water and re-apply the floatant after catching a trout.

- If the wind is carrying down a dense hatch it is often better to go at it from the middle reaches of the lake/loch rather than at the lee end. You can cast across the wind and present the whole outline of the fly to the waiting trout. From mid station you have a much better chance of hooking a good one.

NYMPH FISHING

It could be said that nymph fishing is really just wet fly angling slowed down and executed with a more specific range of flies. Whereas wet flies can imitate anything from a shrimp to a small fish and from a drowned winged insect to a capsized beetle, artificial nymphs largely imitate only one thing. Trout feed avidly on nymphs even when there is an obvious natural surface hatch going on. It is all a question of abundance and ease of access to the food supply. Nymphs are normally plentiful at most times during the year and trout will actively bottom grub for nymphs especially large juicy ones such as the stonefly nymph. Most nymphs are at their most vulnerable when they are making their ponderous way to the surface. The angler should aim to position a nymph imitation roughly at the depth he/she thinks the fish are feeding on the natural.

Nymph fishing was mainly pioneered by Skues and his followers though do remember sparsely tied wet flies which could indeed resemble nymphs, have been around for a lot longer. Though originally some nymphs were made to sink faster by adding copper wire, today a variety of metals including tungsten are used in order to vary the depth. This style of angling is particularly useful on hard, bright days, in calm water and in the cool early and late season when trout seem to be lying low.

BASIC NYMPH TACTICS ON RIVERS

- If you take it that the first way trout recognise their prey is by the way it moves in the water, fishing the nymph is usually only successful when your retrieve is done in a way that matches the naturals' stuttering movement through the water. Nymphs rise and fall in a slow struggle to reach the surface, they do not travel at fast speeds akin to a small darting fish. Though some types of natural nymphs are referred to as 'agile darters' there is no comparison. The speed of your retrieve must match the often laborious rate of the natural.

- Nymph fishing can be done on floating line and long leader, sinking or inter-mediate. Do not equate nymph fishing only with deep water angling, nymphs generally favour the more fertile sheltered margins. Use a line which suits the local habitat.

- Nymphs can be fished singly, as a well spaced team of two or three, or as a point fly on a traditional wet fly team. River nymphs are normally used in sizes 12 to 16.

- You can cast your nymph either upstream or across and down, there are no hard and fast rules but do aim to get the fly into likely trout feeding areas.

- Keeping control of your line and in touch with your nymphs is the key to success as it is in most styles of river angling. Fish the nymphs with a raised rod tip and if a trout touches react quickly and strike or he will have had time to spit your fly out.

- Personally I find nymphs most useful when conditions are looking at their most hopeless particularly in bright, hot sunshine or high water, bleak wintry days. Use a heavy nymph on the point or a top dropper (where it acts like a fast sink anchor) and put on a more traditional one like a Hare's Ear or Pheasant Tail as its partner. Fish them slowly and patiently.

- Tungsten nymphs and other 'heavies' such as Czech nymphs are fished on a short line and roll cast upstream in the current. The nymphs are close to the

Keep in touch with those nymphs as they trundle down on the current

bottom and fished on a raised rod tip. The idea is to fish a small area of the stream and then advance upstream and try again. While the technique (sometimes called the Rolled Nymph) looks incongruous it is highly effective and winkles out trout from seemingly impossible situations.

NYMPH TACTICS ON STILLWATER

- There is often a confusion between so-called nymph fishing for rainbows and what is normally used for brown trout. Nymphs for brownies tend not to be of the shiny bright variety, that is not to say a wild trout might not have a go at say a big Montana Goldhead Nymph but to me these things are lures not nymphs.

- Further confusion exists when trout anglers refer to fishing buzzer nymphs. Buzzers are flies specifically designed to imitate adult hatched midges. Buzzer nymphs are supposed to represent midge pupae which occur below the surface. Thus if the artificial buzzer is fished sunk it is sometimes called a buzzer nymph but strictly speaking it is a midge pupae.

- As on rivers, stillwater nymph representations can be fished singly or in

73

teams of two or three. Sizes vary from 10 to 16. Use floating or intermediate line according to local depth of water.

- Nymph fishing in stillwaters requires a slow and patient retrieve and the nymphs are best fished on a longish line. Cast out over likely trout feeding areas and count to twelve (deeper water fifteen) before retrieving. You can use a gentle raising and lowering of the rod tip to achieve a lifelike rise and fall of the nymphs.

- In stillwaters nymphs are particularly effective in bright sunshine, calm conditions and also early and late in the season when the trout are not surface feeding so much.

- Remember that sometimes tungsten or Czech nymphs are too heavy for use in shallow lochs and stick annoyingly on the bottom. This is because they are designed for use in fast river currents. Balance the weight of the nymph with the depth of the water.

- The only real disadvantage I have found with nymph fishing on stillwater is that it is a rather boring and cold pursuit if no fish are taking. Because it all takes place below the surface it is vital to do your water feature homework well in advance in order to ensure you are actually casting over likely trout holds.

When stillwater nymphing do your homework in advance on likely trout holding areas

TROUTFISHER'S TOP TIPS ON FLEXIBLE FISHING TECHNIQUES

1   Avoid becoming trapped in any one particular method, adapt techniques, fly choice and line selection according to prevailing conditions. Remember nothing is written in tablets of stone.

2   If you see trout active on the surface, use a dry fly. If rises are sporadic try a wet or wet/dry combination. If little or no fish are visible try wet fly and/or nymphs. Go with the flow rather than doggedly sticking to one technique.

3   Whatever tactic you choose aim to get your fly over the most likely areas for feeding trout. Always have the thought uppermost in your mind that trout need food and shelter in order to survive. Fish are always going to be near water features that offer these vital ingredients.

4   Consider fly size as much as its colour, going down or up a size will often work when using standard local dry or wet patterns which you know from experience are normally successful.

5   A floating line can be used with any fly – wet, dry or nymph. Intermediate or sinking lines are useful to gain depth but remember you have to draw the bulk of the line back up to the surface before lifting off, a process which tires the arm after a while. Personally I prefer different weights of flies on the easier worked floating line.

6

THE TROUT AS A QUARRY

'In terms of numbers fishing for it, the common trout is the most important fish that swims'
P. D. Malloch

Over the years there has been a great deal written about how to fish for trout in terms of casting, tackle and techniques. So much so that you would be forgiven for thinking that everyone must now sing from roughly the same song sheet – nothing could be further from the truth! From long experience of listening to other anglers I can honestly say the spread of different views and opinions on how to fish for trout is as wide as ever. Equally the depth of knowledge about wild trout as a quarry varies wildly across the UK. Whether we like it or not, all success in our fishing centres around our knowledge of the fish and their behaviour. Even if you can cast like a dream, can afford the best rods money can buy and talk shop with the best of them in the bar after, if you haven't bothered to study your intended catch you will forever rely on the trout being free rising and on song. Considering that perhaps a maximum of two days out of seven are fishing potentially good 'fishing days' this leaves an awful lot of time for catching nothing!

Despite this some fishermen make the decision to learn little more about trout than what is written on the day ticket – i.e. this water contains brown (or rainbow) trout and is fly only. That is the angler's loss and the trout's gain. Perhaps this lack of enthusiasm for natural history comes from the fact that some text books on trout, as opposed to trout fishing, tend to be dry reading but for the most dedicated. To get round this I shall deal with wild trout behaviour with a fishing-related approach. First let us look at our quarry as a genus for different types of trout will behave in different ways and ultimately this will affect your approach in fishing for them.

TROUT – THE SPECIES

For those of you not familiar with the terminology, all migratory and non migratory trout of the UK except for our American import rainbow trout, fall into the category *Salmo trutta*. Some trout with access to the ocean will show sea going tendencies (sea trout) while trout in inland waters are the brownies of this world. While sea and brown trout are the same species, because of slightly different behavioural characteristics, fishermen will make distinctions in angling

There are critical distinctions between stocked wild and native trout

for them. There is an extensive range of colloquial names for brown trout including lake trout, burn trout, brownies, red or yellow trout, breck (from the Gaelic 'breac' meaning trout) bull trout, ferox, slob trout, Leven trout, parr marked trout, gillaroo, and/or Sonaghen. Sea trout are also known by various appellations including herling, finnock, peal, sewin, white or grey trout. More critically there are also further distinctions regarding stocked, wild and/or native fish.

- **Stocked trout** are grown in captivity from egg stage to eventual release into an aquatic environment.

- **Wild trout** are fish which naturally reproduce in the wild but may have already been cross bred with stocked trout. Because of frequent and often over zealous restocking efforts, the bulk of brownies caught in the UK are of this type.

- **Native trout** are genetically intact unadulterated strains of fish which relate to the original trout colonies of the UK resident since the last Ice Age. They have a set of survival characteristics unique to their specific habitat be that lake or river.

Trout can be classed according to their habitat i.e. East or West coast strains.

- **East coast trout** relate more to the 'Leven' fish and these have silvery coats, show migratory tendencies and favour open water habitats. They are an athletic fish and when caught they often leap and/or tail walk in spectacular fashion.

- **West coast trout** relate more to the rather dour territorial ferox with its deep gold sheen and distinctive blue/green shimmer on the gill cover. When caught they head down to what they see as safety in their habitat and fight strongly with a considerable amount of head shaking and tail slapping.

Though sophisticated, genetic fingerprinting has highlighted these different characteristics, stock movements and natural migration have made these distinctions difficult to isolate exactly. The classifying of trout according to wild or native is essential in planning long term conservation of rare stocks of trout within the UK. Many unique populations of trout have already been lost but we can still preserve the remaining 'strains' if enough effort is made. If genetic testing proves conclusively that we have unusual trout populations still in existence this paves the way for better conservation under the banner of biodiversity. Sadly in real terms very little cash is put into such research projects as many anglers do not see this as a way forward in trout conservation preferring to go along with today's status quo of stocked fisheries.

Several investigations in the UK and abroad are looking at how stocked trout and resident trout interact as in the past very little thought appears to have been given to the effects of rampant restocking. Contrary to misguided but still popular belief, stock additions do not necessarily alleviate anglers' problems in hooking wild trout. In some cases it may actually increase them. Andy Walker well known fisheries scientist and an 'Oracle' even though he would blush to admit it, points out the following regarding the behaviour of stocked trout when introduced amongst naturalised ones.

In general stocked trout can be expected to fair worse than wild counterparts because of lack of conditioning to environmental hazards including predation and territorial acquisition. Trout from many generations of domestication are especially tame. Stocked browns may seem aggressive when compared with wild fish of similar size because they have remained in close shoals in captivity and are prepared to feed openly on the surface. Wild fish on the other hand will always stay close to natural cover and keep away from one another if possible. Because stocked trout compete openly with each other for food while in tanks, they appear more likely to be caught first by anglers or predators like diving birds. There is evidence that stocked fish do not survive as well as naturalised fish in the wild so they do not appear to be able to out compete wild trout in terms of feeding. However when stocked and wild fish are forced together in a limited amount of natural rearing space (as in hefty restocking of small stillwaters) the abundance of the original wild population is likely to decline, sometimes sharply.

In laymen's terms what this means is that by over zealous stock additions you can irreparably alter the character of a trout water. Anglers should remember that once intensive stocking has begun, in future years you will be catching less and less genuine wild browns and more and more introduced stockies. You should therefore proceed with extreme caution if you are about to restock a wild fishery and try to use only local bloodlines if possible.

Wild fish will always stay close to natural cover

A WORD ON THE 'EDUCATED' TROUT

It is always something of a puzzle to read or hear modern anglers talking of trout in terms of high intellect. Trying to catch an 'educated trout' is still a phrase coined by many anglers and it is an odd one. The mind positively boggles as to where the trout got its education. Eton, Oxford, the University of Life or just some boring old Technical College? Yes trout have abundant instincts for self preservation, which includes an urge to feed selectively as much as an urge to hide from predators, but to claim a trout has a thinking analytical brain of human proportion is downright silly. Unfortunately, pick up any angling magazine today and somewhere in it there will be a reference to this super being, the 'educated trout'. Never mind the fact that anglers sometimes fail to adapt and fit themselves in with fish behaviour in a specific environment. The reason we failed to catch that trout is simple, it escaped because it had an education!

So how did this odd phraseology come about? Though it could be earlier, 'the educated trout' seemed to take on real countenance when the cult of dry fly purism took hold. We know Halford and his obsessive followers claimed upstream dry the only way to catch fish, but the theory also prevails that a fish deceived by a dry fly was somehow better i.e. more 'educated' than one caught on the wet. And Halfordians were not the only ones to think their methods caught smarter trout. Nineteenth century Scottish doyens like W. C. Stewart and Tom Stoddart also muttered darkly about the poor showing of loch trout over river fish. Both luminaries argued long and hard that stream trout were much more difficult to catch than loch-bred fish. Naturally this made river trout appear infinitely smarter than the trout of stillwaters. Instead of encouraging the belief that all trout are extremely unpredictable creatures of instinct with a brain the size of a lentil, the image of a trout with at least a Bachelor of Arts degree has been positively encouraged. Trout not with attitude but with an education were well and truly born by the late nineteenth century and have remained with us ever since.

It could be argued that anglers who fail to use their own brains to catch trout, immediately make out the fish has a correspondingly superior intelligence, but perhaps that is a little cruel. To improve catch rates it might be better, instead of thinking in terms of brain capacity, to consider the trout's weaknesses. One is a compunction to feed for however short a period each day. Another is the fact that trout are inherently greedy creatures and once engaged in feeding mode they are often tempted by just one more morsel, hopefully your fly. Dominant larger fish are given to aggressive behaviour and if your fly is well presented to them they will often get in there and snatch it first before their companions get a chance. Equally a fly which is not scary, i.e. one that looks and moves in a way vaguely resembling something a trout might eat, goes a lot further than one which is presented like a pebble in the pond. Wild trout can be devilishly unpredictable and cautiously elusive but learned scholars, I don't think so…

Dominant fish are aggressive and will often snatch your fly first before their companions get a chance

THE FACTS ABOUT TROUT

Having looked at trout as a species and whether they can become 'educated' or not, let us assess the hard realities around which all our fishing is based.

1   All trout have three basic requirements for survival. They need to eat, have a place to shelter and somewhere to reproduce. If they have lots of food and a safe refuge from predators and/or fast currents and stormy weather they grow well, too much reproduction however can mean a reduction in the average size of fish if the competition for food becomes intense.

2   Trout may be athletic-looking fish but they actually thrive best in a stress-free environment. Never mind lean and mean, give them the quiet secretive life anytime!

3   Trout will develop territories which they will patrol and defend with vigour. In general terms the bigger the fish the bigger and more productive will be its territory.

4   Wild/native trout have strong instincts for self preservation which means they reject and/or swim away from anything threatening. Mature, naturally developing trout i.e. trout of 1lb plus which were born and still reside in the wild have finely tuned these instincts, though they are not as uncatchable as some might suggest.

5   Trout will take any fly providing it stimulates either aggression, curiosity and/or a feeding response. However, they will go through periods of inactivity particularly when conditions are unfavourable in their environment for example in extreme heat or extreme cold.

6   The key trigger in sustaining the feeding response is abundance. A big hatch stimulates trout to feed, a minor hatch may work or it may not.

7   Trout can behave differently according to their genetic make up. The original colonising trout of the UK developed genetic characteristics for survival in their patch, it is only with restocking that these characteristics have been diluted. Today trout behave more according to their surroundings and the prevailing conditions, for example clear waters with little cloud cover overhead make for generally shy, cautious trout.

8   Trout develop 'pecking orders'. The most aggressive trout, and these are not always the biggest fish, guard their feeding territory with zeal, patrolling it regularly and repelling interlopers. Lesser trout move up the hierarchy into the better territories held by the bossy trout as and when the fiercest are caught or die of old age.

9   Brown trout as well as sea trout show migratory tendencies. While the sea going trout heads for the briny, the brown trout will still move around its territory sometimes travelling several miles to spawn in the natal stream. Sudden lush food sources also attract trout from some distance away.

81

10 Wild trout do not shoal though they do gather together in some number in preparation for running spawning burns and when an abundant hatch appears. Sea trout are a shoaling fish but that is more for self preservation while in their oceanic phase.

11 Trout reside in clean, well oxygenated water with a reasonable food supply and some shelter. They cannot survive at all in a polluted or extremely acid environment and do not thrive where there is no access to gravel-based spawning streams. Supplementary stocking may be necessary in the latter case though careful assessment should be carried out before rushing in order to avoid making a fishery simply a 'put and take'.

12 A balance in aquatic plant life is important for trout. Weeds provide cover and allow important trout food such as freshwater shrimp to flourish. Too little weed gives a sterile, uninviting environment, too much can lead to a deoxygenation of the water.

13 It is not all science. A little bit of happy coincidence goes a long way in trout angling. Sometimes you catch the trout of your lifetime because you and he were there in the same place at the same time. You were fishing and he was feeding, it is that simple.

It is not all science

Natural spawning should be carefully monitored

SOME FALLACIES ABOUT WILD TROUT …

Trout are cunning educated beasts, hook shy and capable of responding to our efforts with human-like thought and deed Though you might well think this, it is rubbish. We are the interloper in the trout's world trying to rationalise behaviour which usually cannot be based on human reasoning. What a trout does may not seem sensible to us but it does to another trout.

Matching the hatch is essential for success in trout fishing Not really. As long as your fly fishes in a lifelike-way, is not threatening in any way he might have a go at it. Trout however do not necessarily differentiate between similar look-ing flies like an Adams or a Wickham's Fancy. The key is in how you present them.

Trout are more difficult to catch in rivers than in stillwaters Not really, trout are trout wherever they are and both situations can be just as taxing.

There is no such thing as a truly wild trout left in the UK Wrong; while ram-pant stock additions have been going on since the 1800s and many of the traits of these introduced fish are now inbred with cross natural spawning, thankfully not all stocks has been adulterated. There are important pockets of **native** i.e. unadulterated strains of trout still existing.

Where there are no natural spawning streams, restocking is always required for sport No, remember trout can spawn on the bottom of a stillwater where there is sufficient wave action to aerate eggs. It may not be as successful as stream spawning but it can happen. Throwing in more trout is not always the answer and sometimes it will irreparably alter the nature of a water dramatically.

Trout retain memories of being caught and remain shy of anglers' efforts once spooked Not really. If you hook and loose a trout he will *not* return to your fly that day but if he survives he may well be around in a similar spot a week or so later. Memories are short lived in trout.

Trout cannot be caught in certain conditions such as brilliant sun, a thunderstorm, hail or screaming north winds While it is true that lousy conditions make for difficult angling, nothing is impossible. There will often be a 'window' however short in drastic weather and during this time the trout will feed. Often brief windows of opportunity occur during the warmest part of the day.

Ferox trout are large ugly trout with cannibalistic tendencies Not true. If you catch a ferox in mint condition it is a beautiful deep golden fish of perfect proportion. Toothy, lank specimens are ferox which have not recovered from the rigours of spawning. As for being cannibals, ferox feed principally on Arctic charr though they are not averse to the odd trout or two trolled as deadbait.

Trout do not feed in complete darkness Wrong. While it is true that trout take their food because they sight its movement they can also sense vibration in the water along their lateral line and can also smell bait such as worm or maggot even in the dark. Though there may not be as profuse a hatch at night as there is during daylight, the fish will still feed if the opportunity presents itself.

Trout containing worm parasites are in poor condition This is only partly true as parasitic worm infection is a plus factor in indicating a truly adapted wild population of fish with little interference from man. Most trout carry parasites and still provide excellent sport. Unless the infection is very heavy the fish does not lose much condition.

Trout colouration indicates a strain of trout Wrong, sometimes! Colour and markings of trout vary widely within localised populations, partly through genetics and partly through stock introduction. While colour can sometimes indicate a separate strain, it can only be exactly established by genetic testing. Colour is also a camouflage for trout with paler flanked fish normally found in clear water with a light-coloured base and dark trout in dark waters, but it is not universal.

Trout will chase down and kill prey i.e. your flies over some distance Not really – rainbow trout will follow flies but browns tend for the most part to want easy access and will not expend more energy than absolutely necessary to have a good meal. Only during an intense hatch will trout travel upwind/upstream to gulp down the food drifting toward them (see Trout Rises on page 94), most of the time they are too busy guarding their territory.

THE TROUT'S MENU

Trout are opportunistic feeders and can consume a vast variety of insect/invertebrate life as well as molluscs and crustaceans, small mammals, other fish and amphibians. Basically if it looks OK and is not scary to a trout they are likely to have a go at it. Regarding insects, depending on the water you are fishing and also the time of year, the trout might be feeding on any stage from larvae to nymph and from hatched flying insects to spent ones. These will include a wide range of buzzing and fluttering bugs like midges, sedges, mayflies, olives, stoneflies and so on (see also Chapter 8). Microscopic life such as daphnia, tiny creatures only visible under a powerful magnifier, are also happily consumed, along with shrimps, caddis and snails, sticklebacks and minnows, frogs and even occasionally a small water vole or two! If the trout is hungry and the food is a size that he can get his jaws around, then he is likely to have a go at it.

Testing stream fertility

While we will look more closely at feeding patterns of trout in specific environments later in this book, it is important that you understand trout will take advantage of most food items that are in their locale. It is rare for a determinedly feeding trout to reject outright your fly unless it frightens them in some way particularly with clumsy presentation. On the other hand trout which are feeding only sporadically perhaps because of local conditions can be more difficult to tempt.

Factors Affecting Trout Diet

1   **The surrounding environment** In very general terms upland waters will tend to be less fertile and provide less variety of food for trout than those in the lowlands. However there are always exceptions to this rule the best of which I know are in the Scottish Highlands of Caithness and Sutherland. Here there are considerable underlies of limestone mud known as marl and the waters are enriched by alkaline springs permeating up through this marl. The lochs may look dour and acidic as they are surrounded by peat and heather and also in some cases Christmas tree plantations, however do not be fooled by appearances for the feeding is lush and the trout are as fat as butter.

A balance of light and shade makes for happy trout and happy fishers

2   **The pH of the water** Waters which are mineral rich and/or over limestone are normally alkaline and will sustain a goodly choice of invertebrates for trout. Waters which are mineral poor, especially those with a peat base, are less likely to sustain a wide variety of insects and invertebrates. A good indicator of fertility is the presence of freshwater shrimps which only exist in an alkaline setting.

3   **The time of year** Common sense should tell you that the choice of fodder is more limited early in the season, begins to take off from May and reaches a peak around the end of July to fall back again by the end of September.

4   **The amount of daylight** The amount of light on the water has a direct affect on the growth of the local plant and algae life. Waters which are too shaded or enclosed will not receive enough light and trout and their prey may sometimes struggle to become established. Long spells of bright sunlight on open water can cause excessive algae growth and lead to alarming 'blooms'. A balance between light and shade is always best.

CARE AND CONSERVATION OF THE CATCH

While the purpose of this book is to help you catch trout we have an essential duty of care as regards our quarry. Here are a few fundamental steps all of us can take to ensure we do the right thing regarding any trout we manage to attract.

1   When a trout is hooked decide your course of action quickly i.e. are you fishing 'catch and release' or is this one necessary/allowed for the pot? Play the fish according to what you are going to do with it.

2   Use tackle appropriate for the water. Play the trout firmly but not brutally, do not prolong the fight with super light rods and lines which take forever to land the catch and put unwelcome added stress on the trout.

3   Before handling the fish wet your hands as this helps avoids scale damage. Handle trout as little as possible and do not squeeze hard on the underbelly as you risk bursting the swim bladder. Handle the fish over water as much as possible if you intend releasing it, this way if it slips from your hands it will fall back into water rather than down on sharp stones.

4   Use knotless nets to land the fish if you intend keeping it. These again avoid scale damage.

5   If you can use barbless hooks do so as they allow a quick release back into the water without having to lift the trout up. Simply slide your hand down the leader with the trout still in the water, feel the rump of the hook and reverse where the point went in with a backward flick.

6   It is said that barbless hooks can sometimes make a larger entry on the fish's jaw area especially if the fight is prolonged. I personally often have more difficulty releasing trout on barbed hooks especially if the trout has gulped the fly deep in the tongue or upper lip.

7   When returning a trout hold its head into the current or if you are fishing on stillwater submerge the fish and gently rock it back and forward underwater. Both actions get the gills working properly again.

8   You should seriously consider killing any trout which is bleeding profusely at the mouth as its chances of future survival are much diminished. Disease will quickly enter the trout's bloodstream through wounds/ cuts and a quick dispatch is kinder than a slow death.

Return the female trout in late season

9   Put back the female trout in late season (September, early October). These are the ladies carrying the next generation, they will have a fatter, rounded belly, lighter colouration and rounded jaw. Males may be taken if you must, they will have a kyped point on their front jaw and be darker coloured.

10   Take home only what you really need. Leave behind the big bag ethos, do we really need to slaughter trout just for the sake of telling others the numbers we caught?

TROUTFISHER'S TOP TIPS ON TROUT AS A QUARRY.

1   A rising trout is a taking trout. As long as you don't spook him nine times out of ten he will have a go at your well presented fly.

2   As daylight hours increase and temperatures warm, the opportunities for trout to feed also increase and spread out throughout the day. Correspondingly toward the season's end, daylight decreases again and trout feed for shorter more intense periods around the middle of the day.

3   Trout do not sleep as such but go through periods of rest and inactivity usually brought on by changing weather conditions particularly temperature fluctuations.

4   Trout which fixate on one or two selected but profuse food items such as snails or sticklebacks often grow larger than fish which have to forage on a variable spread of insects and larvae.

5   Trout tend to recognise their prey by its movement therefore your flies must fish in a life-like way. This may mean if you are imitating say a sedge you fish a fly with roof-shaped wings in the skittish way of the natural for full effect.

6   Size of fly is often more critical than you may think. Trout prefer something they can get their jaws around without too much effort. However, large trout often take the smallest of flies and I can only put that down to a certain arrogant laziness!

7   Respect your quarry. When handling fish wet your hands first to avoid damaging the scales of the trout. Use barbless hooks if you are intending returning most of your catch, they are easiest to remove.

8   Take home only what you need for the table and follow management guide-lines on what a sustainable catch limit would be for the water you are fishing.

Respect your quarry

7
FINDING TROUT

'We did not see a single "natural rise" all day, yet we caught here and there a trout'
W. Earl Hodgson

Technically, you should be able to find and fish for trout in any clean unpoluted freshwater providing it has angling access. This will include reservoir, loch, lake, pond, stream and river. When faced with an unfamiliar water the challenge can sometimes seem immense even in locating the trout, never mind fishing for them. When approaching the unknown, most of us will want to narrow the odds and go where the fish are likely to be eager to take our flies. Finding trout is one of the perennial problems for all anglers and whether you are fishing still or running water, certain rules will apply. I have detailed these below but must add the caveat that wild trout rarely all 'sing from the same song sheet'.

The first rule in locating trout anywhere is to use your eyes and ears. Fishing is a sensual experience in that in order to be successful you must use all your senses all of the time. Look at the best natural anglers like the heron, diver and otter, they concentrate intensely ever watchful of their prey and what is going on in the surrounding environment. If we can manage even a quarter of their skill we should achieve something.

Use your eyes and ears

FINDING TROUT IN LOCHS/LAKES

When brown trout are the quarry in stillwaters you will generally find them near features likely to provide food and shelter. The following is a rough guide to help in their location.

1   Stillwater trout prefer the margins rather than the cold sterile deeps. In very general terms takeable trout will create their territories in water anything from 1ft to 10ft in depth. Providing there is a source of food, just where the water begins to go from shallow to deep is always a good bet.

2   Trout can lie next to any feature which breaks up the uniformity of the water surface. Thus in stillwater, trout will hole up next to weed beds, islands, beside or behind rocky outcrops, reefs, ledges and drop offs and at inflowing streams. These features create little eddies and backwaters even in the biggest expanses of water.

3   Early and late in the season trout are almost always lying closer to the bank to secure feeding and a degree of shelter. During summer they will forage more enthusiastically at a variety of depths and will spread out across a stillwater as the food supply increases and the margins dry out.

4   Some trout like ferox will lie at depth so as to access their prey. Arctic Char, however which are deeper-lying fish, are only occasionally caught on the fly during the summer months.

5   Late in the season the larger trout including ferox will start to 'migrate' towards their spawning streams and may be intercepted en route as they travel around the sides of the lake towards their natal stream. Larger trout tend to begin this journey earlier than smaller/immature fish.

6   Early in the season big trout may be caught as they linger near in-flowing burns and/or in shallow areas where there is more abundant food. These trout are actually on their 'return route' from spawning and are there to recondition before going back to their deep water haunts.

7   In high summer if the stillwater is fed predominantly from underground springs, the trout may well be found near these as they provide cooler fresh water. Unfortunately these springs are not always easy to locate, however in shallow lakes, circular weed beds often cover the springs and fishing around the edges of these will almost always raise a trout.

8   Unless there is a good spread of bottom invertebrates such as caddis or snail, trout will not normally lie up in environments of 'bald' quality, and pale sand is a good example of poor habitat. Trout may well cruise over sandy bays if the wind-blown terrestrial insect hatch is good but they do not normally favour them as their natural home. Cover from marauders is always a priority for wild fish so you will find them next to those weed beds, islands, promontories etc.

Out on the loch, trout will often hug the shallows early on

9   The biggest trout will establish the best territories and will not move far from these except for spawning purposes or if they latch on to a sudden lush food source appearing in a different sector to their own. Studies have shown that while some trout stick in their own territory for a lifetime, other fish roam freely underwater sometimes over several miles. The reason for this difference in behaviour is not clear but it could be genetic.

10 Observing the activities of the local bird life can also help. Gulls, swallows or house martins busily swooping low over the water into wind and/or flying upstream will mean there is a sustained hatch of insects going on and you can be optimistic that the trout are also steadily feeding in the vicinity just like the birds.

11 Also take a look at the surrounding vegetation. Oak trees, alders and gorse bushes are particularly good homes for insects and trout will linger offshore of these in the hope the wind will blow some of the bugs on to the water.

FINDING TROUT IN RIVERS

Trout in rivers will compete for territories which provide the best amounts of shelter and food. As in stillwaters the bigger trout normally dominate the best territories. There is however the extra pressure of having a current to contend with for though this will bring food and oxygen, spates (times of high water) can cause stress to fish. Bearing seasonal variations in mind i.e. summer often gives low water while early and late season can bring high fast water, trout in rivers will be found near the following:

1   Heads and tails of pools and anywhere where the water gets funnelled down and which concentrates food and oxygen.

2   Below or beside undercut banks, eddies, riffles, backwaters, waterfalls, gravel beds, fences running into water, inflowing streams, submerged boulders and well separated weed beds of Ranaculus or similar. All these river features can act as food traps as well as being places of shelter from predators.

3   Areas of shade where the trout can hide and the cover is best from any predator patrolling the bank for example overhanging trees or banks.

4   Remember trout can be found very near the river bank during periods of flood and spate as they need to secure shelter from fierce currents. Long casting will often spook more trout than it catches in conditions of high water.

Trout can be found very near the bank in high water

5   As in stillwaters, trout will migrate over some distance to reach their natal streams and at different times of the year will be found away from their normal territories so as to access new sources of food.

6   Observing the activities of the local bird life will pay dividends. If the birds are flying and feeding on a hatch the trout are doing the same.

7   Similarly the surrounding vegetation; most trees and bushes adjacent to the water especially if they overhang the bank, make excellent larders and a fat trout or two is likely to be near providing the cover from predators is sufficient.

93

FINDING TROUT BY SIGHT FISHING

Sight fishing in flowing or stillwater (dry fly fishing by any other name) is the most exciting form of trout angling in that you spot a trout rising, creep up on him and cast specifically to what you know is an actively feeding fish. This differs from searching the depths with wet flies though there is still a degree of excitement and expectation about sunk line fishing as you never know when you might be rewarded by that solid thud on the line. Sight fishing is very intense and demands the highest degree of concentration. This is because just as you have virtually given up on that feeding fish, it will suddenly take and you can be caught day dreaming! To assist your success rate in this type of fishing it is a good idea to take into account the differing rise forms you are likely to see...

Trout Rises – Shape and Form

I am a great believer in the fact that if you see or hear a trout rise in any fashion whatsoever, you will have a good chance of catching him with an adroit cast. Anglers will refer to this trout phenomenon as seeing a 'moving', 'taking' or 'feeding' fish, also they may say they 'raised' fish though note it does not auto-matically follow that they caught them! However, it is always worthwhile paying attention to the different rise forms of trout. There is much we can interpret from those blips, swirls, sips, flashes and splashes though do remember to temper your observations with the knowledge that trout will often be feeding as much out of sight as they are on the surface. The following are a few familiar rises which are seen and/or heard on both still and freshwater.

The Boil This type of rise occurs when the trout has determinedly taken some-thing just beneath or on the water surface. The boil will cause not so much a splash but more a prominent whorl and bulge in the water often accompanied by a few bubbles left on the surface. The noise is a resolute 'bloop' sound, the deeper the 'bloop' sound the bigger the fish. Sometimes in clear water you will see the characteristic golden wink of a flank, sometimes you will just be left open mouthed at the distinctive disturbance the trout has left behind. Often the fish will be picking off morsels from a prolific hatch of nymphs, pupae or spent flies. This type of rise is always worth a cast as the trout is in a very intent feeding mode and will usually snatch your fly wet or dry as long as it does not appear a threat.

The Splashy Rise This differs from the boil as it is sometimes a less positive response to whatever food might be available. Trout splash at something on or near the surface which has either aroused their curiosity and/or disturbed them. The trout seems a little tentative rather than going for it in deliberate feeding mode. Sometimes a splashy rise is caused by the trout doing a tail slap on an insect on the water surface. The idea behind this is to drown the insect and take it underneath. Big trout often do this. On the other hand, lightweight splashy rises which make a blip sound often indicate small fish though you should not dismiss them outright as there may be a big boy amongst them. Try a cast or two just in case but do not linger too long if all you contact are small trout.

The Head and Tail This is a slow but dramatic rise when the trout's head comes up, takes an insect and then you see the trout's back as it rolls over the fly in a deliberate fashion. Some anglers will make distinctions between this type of rise and a 'roll' or 'porpoise' action but I think that is splitting hairs. Whatever the description, the trout are taking food from an abundant hatch of insects. If there is more tail appearing than head in the rise (sometimes termed 'tailing') it could well mean the trout are busily feeding on shrimp in which case it is either a 'match the hatch' job or a bright attractor pattern which hopefully diverts their attention. There is not much sound to this rise, it is more detected by sight. A slight pause to let the fish turn down on the fly often assists your catch rate when trout are in this mode but care is required to get the timing right. This rise is always worth chasing for it has similarities to the 'boil'.

The Slash Rise This rise is a made by a trout determined to snatch an insect (often a big sedge or mayfly) off the water surface or just above it. It is a sudden noisy whoosh of a rise which often makes you jump. The trout will appear to raise its body above the water surface and then crash down again pushing out a small wave in front of itself. Because of its violence you will often mistime your strike, however if the trout has not felt the metal of your fly it is worthwhile lifting off quickly and trying to get that fly back near the rings left by the rise. Dry fly is frequently best for trout engaged in this type of feeding. Do not be surprised if you miss as many as you catch as there is a fair degree of unpredictability associated with this type of rise.

A trout rises violently to a surface fly

The Ariel Route This is when the trout leaps vertically skywards straight from the depths apparently to take an insect in mid air. There is not much noise at all during take off, and a hard slapping splash on landing. Again this type of fish activity can leave you agape and you miss the fish either by striking too late or too early. Timing in this case is very difficult. Sometimes the trout are rocketing skyward with the fly already in their mouths and you must strike quickly while they are still in mid air. Fail to do so and they will have rejected your fly by the time they re-enter the water. However at other times the trout are leaping to come down over their prey and you must wait until they have turned on the fly. Commonly seen during mayfly and/or dark olive hatches though note small trout rise like this more frequently than adult fish and your catches may be of immature fish.

Sips and Slurps These are very gentle kiss noises which you can normally only hear on a quiet evening or a very still day. Common during an emerging hatch or fall of small spent insects. A degree of cunning has to be employed during these types of rise as the fish are often obsessively gulping down tiny little morsels and need something to make them change tack. Sometimes it is difficult to judge the size of the trout as only a little bit of the water surface is broken. The intensity of the kiss noise can be a give-away but not always. Definitely worth casting to as the largest trout often take in this very delicate fashion.

'V's or Bow Waves This is not so much a rise as a deliberate charge by the trout at something which looks tasty and/or has invaded his territory. Sea trout often do this when first coming in from salt water into fresh though admittedly they seem more intent in establishing a passage upstream rather than actually feeding. Brown trout are less obvious in this type of action but sometimes can be observed charging down baby sticklebacks by this method. It can be very tricky to make contact with this type of rise and interception is the key. Cast ahead of the bow wave if you can, I prefer wet fly but try anything as the bigger the bow wave the bigger the trout.

Finning or Cruising You can only really see this type of movement when the water is reasonably still. Rather like the 'bow wave' you will see fins break the surface as the trout travels to feed probably on an emerging insect. There is a fair bit of determination in this action and it is sometimes difficult to distract the trout once engaged. You can try an interceptive cast perhaps with dry fly. If the water is glassy but your actions are liable to be highly obvious and your success rate likely to be correspondingly lower.

Travelling Trout This type of rise is a succession of head and tails and occurs when trout move purposefully upstream or travel upwind on the lake/loch gobbling down tasty morsels like hatching olives or mayfly as they progress. It may occur over a distance of only a few feet or a considerable number of yards, much depends on the density of the hatch and the determination of the trout to actively feed. It is always worth trying to get ahead of the fish as this is a positive rise and a good trout may be intercepted. Dry or wet fly will do.

LOCATING TROUT BENEATH THE SURFACE

When no trout are seen feeding on the surface do not make the assumption that nothing is happening in either flowing or stillwaters. 'This water's dead' is a common cry amongst many however more than likely the trout are feeding below the surface. Locating trout is admittedly more difficult when you cannot see anything moving and in this situation you have to rely on your knowledge of where the trout are likely to be in relation to their diet at certain times of the year. For example in the early season trout may well be concentrating on bottom grubbing and picking off stonefly and other nymphs, snails and any shrimp which may be clinging to the edges of weeds. In mid season if the trout are not showing they might well be engaged on amongst other items midge larvae, daphnia or caddis. From August onward the trout may well do a spot of fish fry feeding especially on the newly arrived baby sticklebacks while in September they might feed on small black midge. Remember the Abundance Theory (mentioned in *Fishing for Wild Trout in Scottish Lochs*) in that trout usually take the most abundant food source first and everything else on the menu follows on from that.

Even though the trout are not visible, trust your judgement in that they are not going to be far away from hot spots which provide food and shelter. There is no substitute for local knowledge and observation however and keeping a record of what the trout were feeding on at certain times of the year helps no end in your final fly choice. Whatever the season, it is best to be methodical and work through the range of underwater flies be that wet fly or nymph or a combination of the two.

97

LIMITING FACTORS IN FINDING FISH

While we can narrow the odds by going after trout in likely-looking territories we will still sometimes fail to connect even though we are casting over a place we have secured fish from in the past. Some limiting factors for successful trout angling include:

1   The weather – conditions always affect trout angling particularly the amount of rainfall or lack of it, air and water temperature, wind direction and the intensity of sunlight.

2. The time of year – inland trout will not remain exactly in the same spot day in day out. Though they will have territories they tend to remain mobile to locate food and spawning facilities. Early in the season the amount of microscopic algae the local invertebrates feed on is not well established, trout therefore find their usual food chain interrupted and may hunt elsewhere until things get going.

3   The depth of water – what may have been four feet of water may have turned from lack of rain into two feet or less and to any trout still lying there your intentions are now all too obvious. This applies to rivers and stillwaters.

4   The locale – bald surfaces like flat rocks or sand on the river/lake bed often fail to provide enough food and shelter and are not known for providing good trout territories.

TROUTFISHER'S TOP TIPS IN LOCATING TROUT

1   Your eyes and your ears play a vital role in locating feeding trout, use them.

2   Take time to assess a water and likely fish-holding areas before you start fishing. This pays dividends in the long run, rushing headlong down to the water and starting fishing willy nilly achieves much less though admittedly we are all at one time or another very tempted to do so!

3   A rising trout is a feeding one, keep your profile low, judge your casting distance and then have a go at it as delicately as you can. If the trout is not aware of your actions it may well take your fly even though it is not an exact imitation of what it is feeding on.

4   Bear in mind that all trout have to feed at some time or another, do not be discouraged if you see nothing rising. Go by instinct like the trout do, if it looks a fishy spot with high food availability and is relatively stress free i.e. away from strong currents or bald, brightly lit patches and has some cover from predators, then there might be a fish there.

A rising trout is one which can be caught

8

FLIES TO CATCH TROUT

'Trout will see what they wish to see'
W. H. Lawrie

NATURAL FLIES AND IMITATIONS

While it is not always essential that you match a hatch exactly, there are times when you may be required to do so especially when the trout become picky due to adverse conditions. The best way to go about this is to check the shape/outline of the locally hatching insect and how it moves on or near the water. You may need to spend some time on this as trout are notorious for appearing to be feeding on one insect while actually taking something completely different. A good example of this is during sedge time when the trout may well from time to time slash at these insects but for the most part are actually feeding on something much smaller say a tiny black midge.

Some anglers find the long Latin names for the trout's menu confusing or unpronounceable or both, entomology is not everyone's scene, thus the descriptions of the natural insects you might want to make imitations of are largely by their appearance and colour. Take heart in the fact that trout are not Latin scholars either! Categories to look out for are:

> **Upwinged Flies** This group is very important from both the angler's and the trout's point of view. Amongst others, natural flies like the Green Drake/ Mayfly, March Brown, Iron Blue, Large Dark Olive, Lake Olive, Large Summer Dun, Dusky Yellowstreak, Turkey Brown, Caenis, Pale Watery, Yellow May, Spurwing, Sepia Dun and the Claret Dun/Spinner all fall into this category. Most of the hatched upwinged flies have muted colouration normally being olive green, cream, brown, grey or yellow in colour and they have either two or three elongated thin tails. Once developed from small eggs, the nymphs of upwinged insects can live for up to two years in the water either in burrows (mayfly), in weeds or as bottom-clinging creatures. Though trout undoubtedly take the nymphs underwater, things are at their most exciting when the upwinged flies are first emerging as duns. Trout feed greedily on duns which resemble little upwinged 'sailboats' as they emerge and drift down on the wind and/or the current.
>
> Having dried their wings for one or two days usually clinging on to nearby vegetation, the flies get airborne as sexually mature 'spinners'. They are good fliers and the males will dance in columns above bankside vegetation

trying to attract a female into their midst. If you arrive at a trout water and this dance is in progress you know you are in for a treat! After successful mating the female returns to the water to lay her eggs and she will die shortly after completing the lifecycle. The male may continue to live and mate again but eventually he too succumbs. Now they are known as 'spent' flies and/or a 'fall' of spinners and the trout will take them at will as they lie spread-eagled on the surface.

Classic upwinged fly – the mayfly

When making these flies you should always aim for sound, construction with reasonably buoyant materials. Upwinged imitations are normally fished dry and you want a fly which can stand up to more than one violent take. Make sure the wings are proud of the body so as to retain their upright position in the water. The angler imitating the movement of upwinged flies should go for a slow paced retrieve on stillwater or a dead drift on the river to achieve a realistic copy of these insects.

Roof Winged Flies These are mainly of the sedge family which come in all sizes and include the Little Brown Sedge, Silverhorns, Welshman's Button, the Grannom, Black Sedge, Cinnamon Sedge, Marbled Sedge, Sand fly and the Great Red Sedge. Roof winged flies mainly have a dull coloration, brown, grey and black are the norm. They have four wings, no tails and often have two longish front antennae. They are sometimes called caddis flies as the bottom dwelling larvae of many of this family make protective casings around their body with bits of grit and vegetation. These clever little stone and wood homes are known as 'caddis' hence the name. Note the Alder fly looks very similar to sedge but is technically a different family of insects, however, as an artificial Alder fly is a good imitation for sedge time I doubt the trout notice too much.

When the sedge fly larvae leaves its protective caddis case it ascends to the surface as a pupa which is encased in a loose sheath or shuck. The shuck appears to look like a little shiny air bubble and it is extremely attractive to trout sometimes more so than the hatched insect which flies well and is more difficult to get at. On a still day with careful observation you will sometimes see the little pupa bubble burst and the adult insect emerge. It is worth noting that a slimline wet fly with a bit of flash can often be more successful at sedge time than a big dry fly. Once the 'bubble' splits the adult sedge emerges on the surface. As they struggle to get airborne the newly emerged flies are again vulnerable to trout especially when they skitter across the surface in a semi hopping fashion. This phase often causes the characteristic slash rise (see also Chapter 4) as the trout smacks into the sedge with a bold body lunge. Most roof winged flies are reasonable flyers once in the air and often they will dance together in a dense cloud, rising and dipping at the water's edge. After mating the female lays eggs back on or under the water surface and continues to live for a period fluttering about in the margins before death.

If you want to make dry sedge imitations use materials which give a reasonably buoyant version which sits up well on the water surface. Avoid materials which float so well the trout cannot knock them down, often they simply wish to stun the fly and then take it at leisure. Super buoyant tyings mean the fly pops up too quickly and the trout get suspicious. Do not forget the pupa phase however and make some appropriate wet flies with a silvery flash on the belly or alternatively use some sparkly synthetic fibres sparingly in the make up. Some fly tyers make cased caddis imitations which they fish near the bottom on a very slow retrieve, I personally have not had much success with these but try if you wish. Anglers fishing sedge imitations use a twitched slow to medium paced retrieve to imitate the natural fly struggling on or near the surface.

Caddis containing a larvae of the roof winged Sedge

Flat and Hard Winged Flies Most of the flat winged flies look like houseflies to varying degrees and these include all the classes of midges large and small (sometimes also known as buzzers), most classes of stoneflies, the February Red, the Hawthorn fly and Heather fly (Bibio). Daddies, Black Gnats, Damsel flies and Cow Dung also have wings held comparatively flat above the body. Those flies with narrow wings more folded along the body include Needle flies, Yellow Sally and the Willow fly. The midges have no tails at all while the flies of the stonefly family have either no tails or short stubby ones. Many flat and or hard winged flies are of dull brown/grey hue however there are exceptions notably the damsel which can be bright blue, the Cow Dung is usually yellow and orange and some of the midge family are a distinctive green. In addition some midge larvae, also known as bloodworm, are bright red so bright colours can indeed be used to a degree when fly tying.

An excellent trout attractor – the Bibio

While a hatch of flies like midge and stonefly may not have quite the attraction of say mayfly, they are nevertheless very important especially in less fertile stony regions where they may form a significant part of the trout's diet. Most of these types of insects are rather poor flyers often belly flopping into the water without much of a lengthy flight. All forms of these flies are happily consumed by the trout. When making these flies make sure the overall shape is what you are aiming to imitate with the wings tied along or flat above the body rather than boldly upright. Usually these imitations are fished wet but if there is a prominent hatch of some of the larger flies say of the stonefly family it is worth using a dark dry fly. Nymph and larvae imitations, especially of midges are a popular choice with fishermen hence the name 'buzzer nymphs' which covers a multitude of sparse nymph patterns. Anglers fishing these imitations should use a stuttered slow to slow/medium paced retrieve.

MAKING TROUT FLIES

When tying flies to resemble the natural insects already described, you follow in the footsteps of considerable tradition. The art of making artificial flies has been around since time immemorial and instructions on using specific materials for named patterns (dressings) have been handed down over generations of anglers. Many modern twentieth and twenty-first century trout flies are descended from ancient patterns. The materials you now use may, however, have changed as

103

birds or mammals used in the fourteenth century or earlier like the bustard and the corncrake may have become extinct or are a protected species.

Depending on what pattern you are making you will need materials to make a basic body, hackle, wing, rib and/or tail. Patterns for nymphs are normally the easiest to tie while elaborate upwinged dry flies are usually the most intricate. Wet flies fall somewhere in between. In addition to flies which try to imitate natural hatching insects there is a wide band of flies which do not resemble any natural insect. These are sometimes known as 'attractors' or 'lures' and they are still extremely attractive to trout usually stimulating an aggressive rather than feeding response. Whatever fly you are tying you must combine the materials according to a few basic rules of thumb. These are as follows:

Considerations in Fly Tying

Fly Shape 1 The shape and outline of the fly are its most critical aspects. A fly which does nothing but scare the trout either by being too overdressed and/or hefty is just not going to attract anything. Trout take flies because they vaguely resemble a moving prey of some sort. If your fly sinks to the bottom like a fat round stone it is not going to attract much attention. Flies to imitate insects should be straggly, flies to imitate small fleeing or chasing fish should be shiny and slim with a more stark outline. It is important to note that flies have different shapes/appearances according to where they are in the water. When the artificial fly is first on the surface all the trout see are the points of the hackle and a vague shadow above. Then as the fly penetrates the water surface there is a sudden double take as a mirror image of the fly appears, almost as if there are two flies there. As the fly sinks through the surface film and down its exact shape returns again (try this in an aquarium for further proof!). You should be aware of these properties when making dry or wet flies.

The shape and the general outline of the fly are its most critical aspects

For attractor patterns the colour can be as bright as the dressing demands

Fly Shape 2 When making specific imitations the shape of your fly has to be based on the natural shape of the insect's wings. Thus olives and mayfly with their prominent upright wings require similarly upright imitation wings while sedge imitations should have wings which look like little triangular roofs atop of a narrow body.

Fly Size As a fledgling fisher I never made much attempt to swap fly sizes, I simply stuck with size 10 for lochs and size 14 for river. Now in middle age, hard won experience has taught me that changing down a size in the same trusted pattern will often bring a response where bigger patterns have failed. This is often because the unsuccessful pattern resembles what the trout are taking but is the wrong size to imitate the actual hatch. Remember that smaller flies are often less threatening and when tying favourites you should tie in a range of sizes (normally 10 to 14 for stillwater and 12 to 16 for rivers).

Fly Colour Much has been written about the trout's ability to distinguish colour (it seems they do see a degree of colour near the surface but not as much when the fly is sunk deeply to where the natural light becomes blue/green and the fly increasingly a dull monochrome). Personally if exact fly pattern colours are clearly listed way back to the 1400s I believe there must be something in it. In addition though angling personas like Stewart and Halford scoffed at brightly coloured loch attractor patterns claiming them unnatural and unsightly, it is a fact that nature does indeed have some brightly coloured insects in its midst, for example those blue damsels or bright green midge. Note when you are making imitative flies it is preferable to use blended colours in the body dubbing as this is more like the natural insect. A blend of materials also fits in more with history as tyers of long ago had little in the way of sophisticated materials like Mylar and Glo Brite! However bear in mind that if you are making attractor flies which are designed to stimulate aggression then the colour can be as bright as the dressing demands.

Choice of Materials Before the days of endangered species, flies of fur and feather were made from an assortment of exotic birds and seal fur was in common usage for fly bodies. Nowadays we have good quality substitutes for these however it does pay to check the general durability of materials especially feathers. Some will tear or shred before you have even secured them to the hook so buy the best quality you can afford and do not forget that nature is a great provider of materials. Without paying a penny I collect natural wool from barbed wire, numerous discarded birds' feathers and have been known to deprive the pet spaniel of a few tail strands of her tail.

Floating Qualities for Dry Flies When constructing dry flies which call for a lot of deer hair or elk hair in the wing I recommend lightening up on the amount required. This is because trout often slap at these flies in an attempt to knock them down and take them sub surface. High floating materials like elk hair are almost impossible to submerge and trout can find this unnatural. Use only a few strands or substitute a softer hackle which can be knocked down by the trout.

Light and Air Trapping Qualities The hackles and wings of flies will trap air when they first hit the surface (even wet flies do this when first cast on the water). These little air bubbles will glint in the light and are said to attract fish more so than a fly with a solid body construction. With dry flies you will want to maintain this appearance and floatant is often used, sinking goo is often applied to wet flies to avoid it. It is important to get the balance right particularly in the application of hackles to wet flies – too much hackle and you trap a heck of a lot of air and turn your wet fly dry.

TOP TROUT FLIES

There comes a time when we trout fishers must nail our colours to the mast as regards fly selection. The list I have featured covers many old standards and one or two more modern patterns. Even if you do not tie them yourself it is important to start somewhere and these patterns are recommended and used by many successful anglers. If your efforts fail at the vice these flies are readily available in the shops. As long as the conditions are right, you have the right size and you present them in a delicate way this selection will rarely disappoint! Note a number of the patterns listed are multi functional and can be swapped between river and stillwater though you might need to go up or down a size. This saves time and money if you are on a tight budget.

Troutfisher's Top Six River Wet Flies (Sizes 12 to 16)

Partridge and Orange A sparsely dressed spider pattern which has proved irresistible to river trout for centuries. This simple orange floss-bodied fly with a wisp of partridge hackle is an updated version of the old imitation of the February Red, a natural insect common to many northern and Welsh rivers. The 'P&O' is exceptionally versatile anywhere and could be any olive representation from nymph to spent fly. At a pinch it may even be taken for a shrimp. Often used as a dropper fly rather than on the point.

Greenwell's Glory Made especially for use by Canon Greenwell on the Tweed in the mid 1800s, this fly remains a deadly olive/mayfly imitation as popular on stillwaters as it is on rivers. Many versions of this fly both dry and wet now exist but the original version as described by Courtney Williams in *A Dictionary of Trout Flies* was very simple with yellow silk body well waxed, pale blackbird wing and Coch y Bonddu hackle. Can be used confidently on any stream all year round as a single fly or on dropper or point position and has multi purposes on both still and flowing water.

Gold Ribbed Hare's Ear Nymph A wonderfully versatile general representation of a nymph for use on any river anywhere. Today it has been adapted to dry and loch versions with a wing added but the old simple straggly tying with a body of hare's ear ribbed with flat gold tinsel and well picked out is indispensable. Probably originally tied as an olive nymph but accepted by trout as any nymph struggling to get out of its shuck. Might be sacrilege to suggest it but I think the sunk Hare's Ear is often taken as a shrimp as well!

March Brown Though the natural insect this pattern represents has its main burst of hatches in March and April, the March Brown is a great trout attractor for the whole of the season. Originally tied to represent the natural insect of the same name, this fly can represent sedges, olives, stone flies and just about any other drowned insect you care to mention. Modern dressings have jazzed up the old March Brown but the original is still very effective with its roots set way back in the 1600s. The body is dubbed hare's ear on light brown silk with or without a fine gold wire rib, the tail is two or

River wets

Top row left to right:
*Partridge and
Orange,*
Greenwell's Glory,
*Gold Ribbed Hare's
Ear*

Bottom Row left to
right:
March Brown,
Snipe and Purple,
Black Spider

three strands of partridge and the wing hen pheasant quill feather. Note that the Silver March Brown with its silver body is an excellent all rounder on both river and loch and is particularly effective when fished on the point. Trout probably take the silver bodied version more as a small fish than an insect.

Snipe and Purple Another wispy spider pattern with dark nymph connotations. Excellent during early and late season on fast flowing rivers. The dressing is beautifully simple with a purple floss body and head hackle of the outside of a snipe's wing. The 'S&P' is however one of the few patterns which has not translated very successfully to stillwater use. Why this should be I don't know but it could just be that anglers have followed well established fashion and not used it much on lakes.

Black Spider Though there are now a number of variations on the original version, Stewart's dressing of the Black Spider with brown silk body and sparse hackle of cock starling wing is probably still the best. Simple and deadly it is a drowned insect and/or a nymph and ideal when the trout are taking insects of darker hue under the surface.

Troutfisher's Top Six Stillwater/Loch Wet Flies (Sizes 10 to 14)

Soldier Palmer A superb fly for all trout waters. Can be taken as a shrimp, emerging insect or a drowned one. Also a fly to stimulate aggression. Extremely versatile in any position on the cast but often seen as a top dropper. The oldest dressings date back to the fourteenth century and possibly earlier. One theory purports this fly is named after soldiers returning from Holy Wars who had their paths strewn with palms. Another places it in medieval times when mummers (actors) decorated themselves in palms while a third draws on the fact that hairy caterpillars were once known as 'palmers'. When tying it try and avoid losing the integrity of the fly with too much modern glitz. Should be a fairly stiff hackle which does not collapse on its first wetting. The body is red wool ribbed with fine gold tinsel and the palmered hackle is of ginger cock. Use the rib to hold down the hackle which should run the length of the fly. A red wool tail is often added on modern versions. A couple of extra turns of ginger hen hackle can be used at the head to give extra bushiness to the fly.

Black Zulu Another very old but extremely successful fly. Seems to follow on from the original Black Palmer of the fourteenth century or even earlier. Mainly taken as a struggling insect and usually stimulates a 'smash and grab' response. Fish it fast and watch trout lunge at it or simply draw it in on standard medium paced retrieve and look out for confident takes. Best on point or top dropper. To dress it use a short red wool tail, black wool or seal's fur body, palmered hackle or black cock and rib of fine flat silver tinsel. The Blue Zulu (which fails miserably to represent any natural insect) is nevertheless a very effective fly when everything else is refused. It is valuable in misty conditions when trout are almost impossible to attract and also in dark, dour waters with large trout present

Invicta A great early and late season fly but useful at any time. Mainly a sedge/shrimp imitator but could easily be taken for a small fleeing fish. Invented in the 1800s but still going strong. Some of the more modern variants like the Red Invicta, Orange Invicta, White Hackled Invicta are equally useful. A difficult fly to tie exactly right, it is too sparse and too thin looking, too bushy and it bulks up. The body is best made with picked out yellow seal's fur, rib fine gold twist, body hackle red cock palmered, tail GP crest, beard hackle is a few short strands of blue jay and the wing is of hen pheasant.

Kate McLaren Originally tied as a sea trout fly this is a superb fly for any water. It could be taken for a dark midge or sedge maybe even a shrimp but it is extremely useful at any time. This is a relatively modern fly (early twentieth century) but it is a good one and can be fished anywhere on a three fly cast. Top dropper is often the best. Keep to the original dressing with a body of black seal's fur, rib fine oval tinsel, body hackle black cock palmered in wide spaced turns and add a head hackle in ginger or red hen. The combination of brown and black at the head is what makes this fly distinctive and trout grab it in most circumstances.

Claret Bumble Another modern(ish) fly from the Kingsmill Moore stable and one of the most effective when trout are feeding near the surface. Stimulates a very aggressive response and is highly useful for both sea and brown trout. The dressing is reasonably simple with claret seal's fur body, tail GP tippets, body hackles one claret and one black cock hackle, rib fine oval gold, head hackle blue jay. Excellent as a top dropper and probably now more popular than the Zulu.

Stillwater wets

Top row left to right:

Soldier Palmer,

Black Zulu,

Invicta

Bottom row left to right:

Kate McLaren,

Claret Bumble,

Golden Olive Bumble

Golden Olive Bumble A supremely versatile fly, excellent during mayfly time and also useful for sedge hatches. The exact tying for this is very reminiscent of an Invicta without the wing and it is at its most deadly from May through summer. Not as productive early and very late in the season, probably because it is a fly for the upper water layers rather than a deep sunk wet. I prefer a fly with a greenish yellow tinge but bright yellow seems to do the business just as well. The dressing is body golden olive seal's fur, tail GP crest, body hackle one golden olive cock hackle and one dark ginger, rib fine oval gold, head hackle blue jay.

Troutfisher's Top Six River Dry Flies (Sizes 12 to 18)

CDC Midge CDC dry flies are a delight to use, wispy and delicate yet virtually always capable of floating well in any current. They need only the lightest smear of floatant if any at all. Because Cul De Canard (duck bum feathers!) are relatively new on the fly tying scene, CDCs tend to be used by modern anglers while the old guard tend to stick to their favourites from the past. CDCs are versatile in imitation of midges or just about any struggling small insect trapped in the surface current. When tying these keep them sparse, thankfully the dressing is relatively simple. Body stripped quill from a peacock eye feather, wings two small CDC plumes, head sparse hare's ear tied in with two turns of thread.

Greenwell's Glory (dry) This is a perennial favourite on rivers primarily used for imitating olives but it works for most upwinged insects. Though the original was made as a wet fly this is every bit as effective. For the winged version tie the wings split upright and use a greenish olive shade for the body.

The original dressing was for a body of yellow silk well waxed to darken it, wing blackbird inner (tied upright for the dry version) and head hackle Coch y Bonddu. The dry wingless Greenwell's has yellow silk again darkened with wax, tail medium dark furnace cock hackle fibres, head hackle two medium dark furnace cock hackle. Both are equally effective.

March Brown (dry) Invaluable in most circumstances and though it is meant as an exact representation of the natural, it is useful for most surface hatches from midge to sedge. Though this was originally tied as a wet fly there are a number of useful dry fly variations. I like the hackles on this one as they collapse when a fish takes rather than staying brutally upright. This dressing comes from Courtney Williams *A Dictionary of Trout Flies* where it is called a March Brown Spider which can be 'used as a floater with good results'. Body hare's ear mixed with claret wool. Rib yellow silk. Hackle long feather from partridge back and whisks two strands from brown partridge. Some versions I have used have a grey wool body and these were equally effective.

Iron Blue Dun (dry) A super little dark fly good in most circumstances. Natural 'Iron Blues' tend to be prevalent during early and late parts of the season but really the imitation is useful whenever a darker shade of natural is hatching. The version from the River Clyde has no wings and is as follows. Body peacock quill dyed brown, tail dark brown or grey hackle fibres, hackles two cock hackles with dark blue dun at the head and red game tight in behind it.

Rough Olive A universally accepted dry fly always invaluable during any olive or upwinged hatch, good on river or stillwater. Personally I prefer this version to the Olive Quill which I feel is rather similar to the winged Greenwell's. Highly effective for olives and also green drakes mayfly. Use a good greenish tinge in the body. The dressing is sparse to medium but don't go over the top. Body olive mole, rib fine gold wire, tail medium olive cock

River dries

Top row left to right:
*CDC midge,
dry Greenwell's,
dry March
Brown*

Bottom row left to right:
*dry Iron Blue,
Rough Olive,
Walker's Red
Sedge*

111

hackle fibres, hackle medium olive hen with a shorter black hen hackle directly behind. The version of this fly I often use has a small grey upright wing and it is deadly in our tea-coloured northern rivers on an overcast day.

Great Red Sedge A wonderfully versatile fly with sedge connotations but capable of stirring up trout at any time. Successful on stillwater where it is often tied in large sizes 6 to 10 but smaller 12 to 16 do the business on flowing water. The dressing should be medium, not bushy but not overly sparse. Body grey mole, body hackle palmered dark red cock hackle, rib gold wire, tail red cock hackle, wing brown speckled hen tied roof shaped rather than upright.

Note: The illustration on page 111 is a 'Walker's Red Sedge' which has a denser tying but is just as useful.

Troutfisher's Top Six Stillwater Dry Flies (Sizes 10 to 16)

Wickham's Fancy (dry) A multi purpose dry fly good for olive, sedge or just about any winged insect on the water. Useful on bright days when the gold body seems to attract more attention than dark-bodied flies. Sizes 10 and 12 are better on windy days, smaller sizes are good in calmer weather. There are a number of different dressings for this fly, the wings on mine are grey and tied upright. Here is the version from Courtney Williams' *A Dictionary of Trout Flies*. Body flat gold, body hackle ginger cock hackle, wings medium starling, head hackles two ginger cock hackles. Also mentioned is a whisk of brown red gallina but this can be omitted without the trout noticing.

Rough Olive (dry) An exceptionally versatile fly, nifty for any hatch of prominently winged insects from mayfly to lake olives but can be used when sedge and midge are on the water. Effective with or without a grey upright wing. Larger sizes are good in the top dropper position in broken water and smaller ones can be fished singly in calm conditions. The dressing is as for river dry flies.

Grey Wulff Indisputably the best green drake mayfly imitation for Scottish lochs, floats brilliantly even after several hits. Equally good when the water is apparently dour and wet fly is failing, in fact this attractive mouthful can stir up trout from nowhere. The Grey Wulff was devised by Lee Wulff in the 1930s as an answer to the terribly sparse patterns of that period. Wulff stated that when devising the fly he *'beefed up the body and, needing a better floating material than the feathered tails of the time, used bucktail for durability and strength in both tails and wings'*. The result may be slightly incongruous when set against dainty Greenwell's, but trout do not seem to give a fig and take Grey Wulffs down with gusto. Note the dressing I use has an olive coloured head hackle rather than the blue dun. Tail bucktail, body grey rabbit or angora wool, wing brown bucktail tied upright or split in a V shape, head hackle is a blue dun cock hackle.

Black Hopper (dry) A leggy fly capable of attracting trout in most situations

Stillwater dries

Top row left to right:
dry Wickham's, Rough Olive, Grey Wulff

Bottom row left to right:
Black Hopper, dry Greenwell's, dry Hare' Ear

but probably best used in the top dropper position when there is a chop (wave) on the water. Can also be fished on a slow semi static retrieve when trout are rising to larger insects on the surface. Hoppers are modern flies but have their roots set in traditional attractor patterns. The dressing is normally body black seal's fur, rib fine oval silver, hackle black hen medium dressing not too sparse or thick, legs six knotted black pheasant tail fibres.

Dry Greenwell's Just as good for loch trout as it is for those of the river. Useful when fished in small sizes in semi calm conditions. Can be taken as a green midge, small olive or even a beetle. Extremely versatile in conditions of light breeze. Dressing as the river dry fly.

Hare's Ear (dry) Not technically a dry fly but a successful attractor whenever trout are feeding well on or near the surface. One for any surface hatch but particularly for sedge or large midge. Fish them in breezy conditions on a medium to fast retrieve for best results. Keep the tying simple and light. Body dark fur from the hare's ear, rib flat gold tinsel. Head hackle light furnace hen, wing pale starling.

Troutfisher's Top Three River Nymphs (Sizes 12 to 16)

Gold Ribbed Hare's Ear (nymph) Exceptionally functional nymph for all rivers in all seasons. Has caught trout from the southern chalkstreams to the northern rivers of Scotland. Particularly effective in fast flowing water, the GRHE represents just about any drowned nymph or insect struggling to emerge. There are a number of different dressings for the GRHE but the best I know is from Courtney Williams, *A Dictionary of Trout Flies*. Body dark hare's ear fur spun on yellow tying silk. Rib flat gold tinsel. Hackle strands of body well picked out. Tail three fine whisks of hare fur.

Harelug Goldhead This is a deeper fishing version of the GRHE and is vital for high water fast flowing conditions. Technique for fishing this heavy nymph is a Roll Cast upstream and a trot down not unlike upstream worming. Not really intended to represent anything in particular but highly effective nevertheless. The dressing is simple. Body lighter hare's ear well picked out, rib medium flat gold, head gold bead (different weights can be used, 3mm is popular). I'm not a great fan of Goldheads myself however if you substitute the brass coloured heavy putty for the head you get a more acceptable looking version which does the same thing and sinks like a stone in fast deep water.

Sawyer's Pheasant Tail Nymph Often the most simple patterns are the most deadly and this one is a real classic. This is a vital addition to any fly box as an all round nymph imitation and is suited to rivers and lochs. The original version by Sawyer was nondescript brown, today many anglers go for different colour flashes on the thorax including green, orange, yellow and red. Fish it upstream for best results though I personally think a dead drift across and down works adequately. The dressing is body fine copper wire wound along the hook and then built up to make the thorax just back from the eye of the hook. Tail three strands of pheasant tail. Over body pheasant tail fibres overwound along the hook and built up over the thorax.

River nymphs

Left to right:
*Gold Ribbed
Hare's Ear
Nymph,*

*Harelug
Goldhead,*

*Sawyer's
Pheasant Tail
Nymph*

Troutfisher's Top Three Stillwater Nymphs

Cove's Pheasant Tail Highly effective in bright or calm conditions when trout are being picky. Often favoured over the more spartan Sawyer's Nymph and used to imitate any general nymph. The hare's ear fur in this makes it a supreme trout attractor. Fish it on a slow retrieve for best results. The dressing is simple; body three or four strands of pheasant tail, rib copper wire and thorax of dubbed hare's ear.

Damsel Fly Nymph Although it is meant as a damsel this is an excellent all rounder capable of attracting trout in many differing circumstances from early season to hard bright mid summer conditions. I think that it is the olive green colour of this that really does the business. I tie the simple version

*Stillwater
nymphs*

Left to right:

*Cove's Pheasant
Tail,*

*Damsel Fly
Nymph,*

*Gold Ribbed
Hare's Ear*

without eyes, the heavily dressed versions are lures by any other name and meant principally for rainbows. This dressing is from John Roberts' *New Illustrated Dictionary of Trout Flies*. Tie the body reasonably thick but not bulbous and avoid being too sparse. Picking out some of the seal's fur adds extra dimension. Body pale green seal's fur, rib fine silver wire, legs one turn of olive hen hackle, tail three pale olive cock hackle tips.

Gold Ribbed Hare's Ear Just as indispensable in stillwater as it is in the river. A delight to use in any conditions but probably best in calmer weather when the nymph can be sunk and retrieved slowly. Dressing is the same as the river version.

Troutfisher's Top Three Saltwater/Estuary Trout Flies

Teal Blue and Silver (TBS) I cannot rate this fly too highly as a sea trout attractor and it also does well for any slob or brown trout lingering in tidal water. It has the slimline flash of a small fleeing fish or a sand eel and has in my opinion never been bettered. Almost always I fish it on the point with a dark dropper above. The dressing is classic with oval or flat silver tinsel body, tail of GP tippets, hackle bright blue cock hackle, rib fine silver or gold wire and wing of teal flank feather. Keep the hackle sparse and wispy and fish the fly on a fast retrieve.

Blue Zulu The Blue Zulu is a mystery fly resembling nothing on earth yet it is a supreme taker of brown and sea trout often in poor misty conditions when all else has failed. Make it traditional and reasonably bushy and fish it well sunk and on a reasonably fast retrieve. It is good on a top dropper position above the TBS where it could look like something shrimpy fleeing the apparent small fish chasing behind. Dressing is tail of red wool, body of black seal's fur or wool, rib flat silver tinsel, palmered hackle black cock hackle and a bright blue head hackle.

Breathaliser I found this fly accidentally as it is actually a rainbow trout lure rather like an Appetizer but it works exceptionally well as a streamer fly in saltwater. The colours are ideal for sand eel imitation and while this is the dressing given in John Roberts' *New Illustrated Dictionary of Trout Flies* you can mix and match the streamer wings even going for hair wing rather than hackles. Fish it fast in the incoming tide and watch out for 'smash and grab' takes. The dressing is a body of flat silver tinsel, tail black hen fibres, wings two hot orange hackles overlaid with two green hackles tied long streamer style, collar/head hackle badger and head of black varnish. You can use jungle cock for eyes but I prefer it without.

Saltwater trout flies
From the top:
Blue Zulu,
Teal Blue and Silver,
Breathaliser hairwing

TROUTFISHER'S TOP TIPS ON FLY CONSTRUCTION

1   If you want to imitate a specific insect go by its wing shape/form first i.e. upright, roof shaped or flat winged.

2   Trout recognise their prey by the way it moves in the water. Your fly must be designed to progress naturally on or under the surface, if the construction is too heavy or light the end product may not do the job it is supposed to do.

3   The qualities of light and air are critical when making a fly. For example does the material used have a subtle glitter to it at differing depths or do the hackles of the fly trap air bubbles efficiently?

4   An absolutely exact representation of the natural insect is not always essential. Attractor flies which catch the attention of trout without spooking them can be just as useful.

5   Remember you can make the most beautiful imitation of a natural insect yet still fail to catch trout if your presentation of the fly is too clumsy thereby causing the trout to flee in a flash!

An exact representation of a natural insect is not always essential

9

THE WEATHER AND TROUT FISHING

'Nature is reckless of the individual. When she has points to carry,
she carries them'
Ralph Waldo Emerson

THE CONDITIONS

How many times have you studied the catch return book of a fishery and pondered on why the water you have just spent all day flogging for little reward, had only a month ago produced a succession of trout of two pounds plus? Was their success and your failure down to skill, simply being in the right place at the right time, or the influence of the weather? Probably a combination of all three but the influence of the prevailing weather must be considered paramount. While I can describe best or worst conditions, in the end the British weather is such an unpredictably awkward beast my advice is to at least try to fish even if you only do it for half a day. If you fail to secure trout, then you know what to blame it on!

Trout and the Weather
There are some weather 'constants' which will affect trout behaviour but remember too that there is always a trout out there prepared to break the rules.

1   Trout thrive best in cool well oxygenated water. When there is a prolonged hot spell, the heat causes marginal feeding areas to dry out and waters will lose their oxygen-carrying capacity. Neither effect is good news for trout and they will temporarily retreat to what better conditions they can find: for example in rivers they fall back to the cooler sea or to deeper pools and in lochs the trout linger in deeper, colder but less fertile water.

2   Trout prefer areas of both light and shade within a water. When the sun beats directly down from overhead they will seek shaded areas for example in weed beds, off drop offs/ledges or between boulders. In dull conditions they will often cruise across open areas foraging for any food as they go though they will normally stay reasonably near their own territory.

3   Trout have no eyelids and bright light directly in their eyes will disrupt their vision. Often they will not see their prey as well as they can in dull light. Thus when sun, wind and/or current come from the same direction they will prove harder to attract.

Trout can exist in low temperatures

4   Trout can exist in low temperatures providing the oxygen balance is not disrupted too much. Ice on lakes or rivers does not affect them greatly other than that they tend to slow down a little as food availability is generally lower.

5   Trout appear to be sensitive to the highs and lows of barometric pressure especially if there is a sudden sharp fall on the barometer. Settled conditions are normally more favourable.

6   In stillwaters, trout react to the wind as this carries the oxygen over their gills and brings food toward them like a current. Therefore most trout will face in the direction of the breeze. Trout in rivers react to the wind in similar ways though the flow direction remains their first source of oxygen and food.

7   Trout can make themselves more vulnerable to predators (including fisher-men) while sheltering in shallow waters to escape the icy blasts of the early season and also throughout the year when they want to gain easier access to food which is always more profuse nearer the shore.

8   Very few trout decide life is better out in the sterile deeps. Apart from the Ferox strain which take up a deepwater residence in order to pursue their principal prey the Arctic Char, most wild trout will hunt in the margins. Thus when feeding and/or sheltering they lay themselves open to capture.

Weather Folklore

Many old sayings surround the UK weather, bearing in mind the unpredictability of fish and conditions here is a useful selection of those most applicable to fishing:

Sun before seven, rain before eleven Anon. A fairly accurate saying for early season angling, not so good in summer months when other factors come into play.

When the swallows fly high it is fine, when they fly low it will rain Anon. Don't know so much about the rain aspect but any low flying birds skimming the water surface means a hatch of insects are on and you should get fishing pronto.

Gusty winds before the rain Trad. Usually accurate especially in exposed areas such as high hill lochs. The warmer air is pushed out ahead of the rain clouds and a sudden increase in wind speed will often be experienced before a rain shower arrives.

Dark water, dark fly

If the sheep go uphill it will clear, if they remain on low ground it will continue to rain Attributed to Thomas Best. Only really useful if you are fishing in view of a flock of sheep and there are hills for them to march up and down on!

When the moon is full the trout lie quiet in their holds Rev Daniels, *Rural Sports* Volume II. True to a certain extent. Moonlit nights are normally cold and still and it will be quiet in the trout food line. Then again trout are supposed to hunt by sight!

Old Betty's joints are on the rack, her corns with shooting pains torment her and to her bed untimely sent her from *Signs of Rain* attributed to Dr Jenner and/or Dr Darwin. Approaching rain does strange things to anglers, but then don't we all go to bed like this sometimes?

If Candlemas Day (2 February) is fair and bright, winter will have another fight Trad. Fine February weather does indeed sometimes backfire into a prolonged winter and a late spring.

When clouds appear like rocks and towers, the Earth's refreshed by frequent showers Trad. This is reasonably accurate for Scotland anyway!

When the ash is out before the oak, then we may expect a choke Trad. This refers to an impending drought and could well be true in certain parts of the country.

Clear moon, frost soon Trad. Usually true in winter, good moonlight in summer can also herald clear bright weather during daytime hours.

A settled spell will bode us well Trad. True for both trout and fishermen.

Dull fly dull day, bright fly bright day Trad. Semi useful old angling saying about choosing your fly according to the conditions. Also…

Dark water dark fly, bright water bright fly Trad. Of similar use though in this case bright water refers to its clarity. Annoyingly both these sayings about fly choice can be reversed to good effect thus leaving the angler none the wiser!

Trout will lie off the shore on to which the wind is blowing Anon. The idea behind this is that the trout will await a collection of surface fodder being blown down to them. To be successful the angler must go to this shore and cast into the teeth of a gale, a daunting task the further north you go. Sadly this saying is not always correct as a lot depends on the localised trout population existing along the windblown shoreline. If they are mainly skinny fingerlings no amount of wind can change their size.

Cold, wet, misty and altogether beastly – no fish rising from Muriel Foster's Diary, *Days on Sea, Loch and River*. Just about sums it all up!

Rainfall

Rainfall controls many factors in a trout's life including how well they survive as babies in the spawning streams (too much rain causes spates which can wash out eggs, too little of it and redds dry up). Trout fry may spend around two or even three years in the natal stream and if this suffers from lack of rain they may find their lives under threat from lack of shelter, lack of oxygen and lack of abundant food supply. Mortalities are very high at this stage of a trout's life. Once in the main river trout will have become hardier but nevertheless lack of rain will cause their usual feeding and sheltering areas to dry out placing added stress on the fish. Equally, excessive river spates will pressurise the trout into seeking hidey holes out of the fierce flow. In general, however, river trout benefit from heavy rain washing extra food down the stream. Providing the water does not overload with deoxygenating silt which can cause mortalities, rainfall is almost always beneficial.

A considerable amount of rain can have an equally useful effect on stillwaters as raised overspills of water enrich the food supply and trout can forage in new larders. Sometimes if the rain is heavy but not prolonged it can produce a thin layer of cold water on the surface of a stillwater. It is said that this can some-

Checking the spawning stream

times lessen the frequency of the fish rising though personally I think it doubtful. Conversely a lack of rain causes margins in stillwaters to dry out and fish to seek deeper water.

The Solunar Effect

The moon's effects on brown trout are more subtle. Moonlight has a habit of stirring up all sorts of raw emotions in fish, from the need to feed to the need to produce offspring. It is thought that trout feel the first urges to make ready to spawn after the September yellow harvest moon appears, and that the first spawning migration will often occur in late October after the full moon. However lunar influences are thought by some to go back much further, right to the receding of the last Ice Age when the trout first colonised the UK. If all trout were at one time saltwater bound, predisposed to the moon and the tides, there is a likelihood that they could retain some ancient memory of their principal feeding times – high and low tide. We are talking about deeply embedded genes here. Consequently some anglers believe the 'solunar' theory still holds water and serious consultations on tidal times are sometimes seen at the waterside, even when the trout are being hunted well inland in freshwaters without a link to the sea. I do not have strong views on this although I have noticed when fishing for trout on my local river that in summer the fish come say a mile upstream and fall back according to high tide times. This pattern occurs even when the trout are in fresh rather than brackish water and are lying a fair distance from the river mouth.

Barometric Pressure

Anglers should never overlook barometric pressure. As a 'high' arrives the air pressure on the water increases and the water surface absorbs more oxygen. This in turn makes more oxygen available for respiration purposes which stimulates activity in trout. Conversely when a 'low' comes in air pressure decreases, oxygen is given off from the water surface and trout may respond to this by going deeper and lying quiet for a while. Though it is difficult to prove these effects conclusively, all evidence points to the swim bladders and lateral lines being highly sensitive instruments giving the impression that trout can sense weather changes a heck of a lot quicker than anglers can. It certainly puts a whole new perspective on the saying 'I can feel it in my waters'!

When the barometer is in a settled pattern be that a high or a low then the fishing tends to be better than when there is a sudden plummeting low. Checking the barometer before you go is the only way of proving this and from experience I can say this theory has some grounding.

The Effects of Global Warming

Portents about the future effects of global warming are often alarming. As our world heats up all sorts of predictions are being made, some realistic, some fanciful and some downright scary. It seems that in years to come, rising seas might engulf the lower-lying coasts of Britain, some of our agricultural land will turn to desert, winters will be stormier and summers much drier. It now also looks very much as if the UK will split in two in terms of climate with the North and West coast becoming increasingly wet and stormy throughout the year, whilst the South Eastern half of Britain becomes considerably drier in the summer months. And as if all these changes were not enough, the weather itself looks likely to become more and more unpredictable with sudden rapid swings in both temperature and rainfall leading either to drought conditions and/or flash flooding prevailing, depending on where you live.

These 'feast and famine' weather situations are often attributed to global warming and its associated 'Chaos Theory' and as time passes they look set to deepen in intensity. The warning signs are already there. Our winters lack the snow of the 1950s, 1960s and 1970s which means there is considerably less snow melt to top up our streams. Instead winters are often warmer and wetter with unexpected dramatic floods occurring in lowland areas. Summers are today much more extreme, swinging from hotter and drier to colder and wetter in random fashion. The UK's native and introduced fish do best in a stable habitat of cool clean water yet now and in the future, their security is likely to be increasingly destabilised not to say put in peril as the Chaos Theory led by global overheating takes a firmer hold. Today the UK's fish populations are having to deal with increasingly volatile weather patterns with flash floods wiping out their natural spawning habitats in the winter months and in summer, plummeting water levels from lack of rain cause droughts which expose and destroy natural feeding areas close to the bank. More and more the fish are driven away from their territories in the shallows and out into deeper more sterile environments were food is much scarcer.

Increases in world temperature bring many problems

Increases in temperature bring many other problems, burgeoning weed growth in already fertile waters being just one. Rivers in particular become totally choked up and remember too that with rising temperatures there is a corresponding increase in microscopic algae. Should your local stillwater develop blooms of blue green algae you may find it closed down as this algae (which looks like dots of blue and green paint shaken into the water) is toxic to humans and animals. Also as our climate warms up so our freshwaters lose their oxygen content and every year we read of angling venues losing their entire fish stock from deoxygenation. Heat also increases the prevalence of disease amongst fish particularly from parasites which flourish in warm climates. Fish deaths directly attributable to changing weather patterns were commonplace in the 1990s, one can only guess what will happen thirty years from now if global warming really takes hold.

You might think that the prediction that the North Western seaboard of Britain will become wetter will save some fisheries from extinction especially if all our East coast rivers collapse in drought conditions but unfortunately it may not work like that. If as purported, the increased rainfall is accompanied by storms, floods and high winds, then the security of young fish fry, is greatly threatened and older fish may also become over stressed with their normal resting stations in quiet pools mercilessly swept away in savage currents.

It looks therefore that in my dotage, I will have a choice of two angling venues. I can stick to the East where I can don shorts and a T-shirt and go fishing for little or no fish as there will be no water for them to dwell in. Alternatively I can head out West wearing my full waterproof regalia and angle for fish that may (or may not) be there and risk being drowned in a flash flood! Neither of these prospects look attractive and I for one will continue to make noises about global warming in the future. My conscience will not allow me to leave such a legacy for my children.

CONDITIONS TO TRY AND AVOID WHEN TROUT FISHING

1   Thick mist. While it is not impossible to catch trout in mist, sometimes you can nail them with a blue fly like the Blue Zulu or a whitish fly like a pale Loch Ordie, mist has an oddly deadening effect on both flowing and still water. Fewer hatches occur in a shroud of cold mist and also the opaque white light seems to 'blind' the trout and they appear to have difficulty in seeing your fly.

2   Thunderstorms. Not because the trout don't rise, they do and often quite furiously, it is just you make a wonderful lightning conductor standing in water and waving a long carbon fibre rod around!

3   Severe gales with 'Cats' Paws'. Apart from the obvious difficulty for the angler in standing upright, severe turbulence on the water surface which causes the water to spatter and break up into 'Cats' Paws' can cause the trout to go deeper where they can sight their prey easier. Your fly/flies are just a blip in a maelstrom and trout may not take them as readily. I have caught trout in such gales but it is not pleasant and is not recommended for the beginner.

TROUTFISHER'S TOP TIPS FOR READING THE WEATHER

1   The best trouting weather is nearly always dull, mild and cloudy with a reasonable breeze blowing. On average a maximum of two out of seven days will be like this one with one 'perfect' day in seven quite the norm. When it is happening you must take full advantage of it, the odds on catching trout are that much better in these conditions though nothing can ever be fully guaranteed.

2   The odd swift shower of rain also helps stir things up by activating a goodly hatch of insects to make the trout rise with gusto. Wind and rain are important climatic by-products for they can stir up all sorts of goodies from the loch or river floor and a veritable fishy banquet results.

3   Only extreme conditions, notably excessive heat, can cause real grief for mature trout, however young developing fish are vulnerable to heat, cold, frosts and spates.

4   Check the barometer before you go, look for settled, even conditions rather than plummeting lows.

5   Remember that you should always give it a try no matter what, just occasionally you will be pleasantly surprised.

Young trout are vulnerable to extremes of heat, cold and rainfall

10

INTRODUCING YOUNGSTERS TO TROUT FISHING

'Not to transmit an experience is to betray it'
Elie Wiesel

It may not be too obvious to hardened trout fishing aficionados, but the sport of angling is now officially in decline. Though it might not appear so when out on the local water on a Saturday, numbers taking up fishing have dropped significantly over the last ten years and the trend looks set to continue. At one time fishing sat atop the outdoor pursuits tree in terms of numbers participating, now according to latest government figures detailing those taking part in outdoor recreation, it barely creeps into the top ten. All right, so we might be tempted to sit back and say 'goody goody – more fishing for me' but to do so will not make the future any brighter. Fewer young anglers with their fresh ideas and boundless enthusiasm means an increasing loss of angling tradition. We have already seen that these traditions stretch back to at least the fifteenth century and if no new blood comes into the sport, angling customs will eventually stagnate.

In the twenty-first century we now have fewer voices able to speak out when wild fish stocks take another of their frequent nosedives and even less clout in dealing with government policies which put fish conservation way down the list of priorities. With an ever reducing amount of new recruits coming in, the angling banner is left to be carried predominantly by what marketing men call the 'grey market' i.e. fisherfolk most of whom are not getting any younger!

So just why has this decline become so marked? The answers are as much linked with the way our society has evolved as they are with public perception of the sport. Our contemplative 'gentle art' sits uncomfortably on the back of a world of Internet superhighways, mobile phones, satellite communications and instant access to all things shiny bright. Today the children we would hope to introduce to fishing seem to prefer computer animated games and/or the contorted world of satellite television where everything happens at full volume (or am I the only one who thinks everyone shouts all the time on these channels?). Fishing by its very nature is a quiet uncomplicated outdoor pastime demanding patience, a fair degree of skill and a deal of magnanimity in coping with failure i.e. not catching! Quick adrenaline fix youngsters are finding the attributes of angling less and less appealing. Why struggle against the elements to catch often uncooperative wild fish when you can play a computer game, save the universe, pulverise enemies and talk on your mobile all at the same time. Fishing has all but missed the boat in the techno-age, its pace is not hip and its image is not hitting the 'cool' spot.

Even when national fishing organisations try and reverse this alarming trend they can find their paths blocked either by lack of funds and/or by having to divert all their energies into fighting ever more serious battles to save game fish stocks. Sadly, as we struggle to defend fish from anything from high seas drift netting to fish farms and from seals to global warming, our apparent persistent moaning tends to create a very negative image around ourselves. Who then wants to be part of the show if the overall quality of angling is deteriorating as rapidly as we make out. And if that is not bad enough, in certain areas of the UK we also have to face flak from extremist animal rights campaigners who view angling in a perverse bloodsport light. Talk about a no win situation – trout fishing's very own Catch 22!

We need to spend time encouraging youngsters into the sport

So what can we do to bring more youngsters into the sport? Short of decamping ears from mobiles and permanently switching off the flickering screen(s), probably not a great deal for some I fear! But maybe that's unkind. If I and many like me grew to love the sport after my late Dad's first initiations, then there must be others who can and will develop the same passion given a little encouragement. For the sake of the sport's future we have to try and there follows a few helpful tips on initiating youngsters into trout angling:

Simple Advice for Teaching Tyros

- Fly fishing is a wonderful pastime for children, providing you introduce them to it in the right way! Spending hours showing them your beautiful casting technique while they shiver and finally lose interest on the bank will achieve little except alienation.

- The ideal age for children to start fly fishing is from about nine upward, below that their attention span is too short and their physical strength is often not up to wielding a long rod for any length of time.

- The whole experience should be broken up into enjoyable segments, children generally do not want a university syllabus on how to fish, they just want to get out there and do it. A good lunch complete with fizzy drink and vile smelling crisps like cheese and onion, goes down a treat.

- Go fishing on a dull, warm, breezy day which will offer the best chance of catching a trout. Avoid extremes in weather like thick mist, icy cold, strong winds or strong bright sunshine with no cloud cover.

- Initially if you have complete novices with you, choose a water which has lots of average sized free rising trout rather than one which has small numbers of very large difficult fish. As a rule stocked ponds offer better odds than wild waters but avoid creating the wrong impression i.e. every time you cast, a fish of 2lb plus will impale itself on the fly as this rarely if ever happens in the world of wild trout angling!

- Use light tackle. Use a 9ft rod, floating line and 4lb nylon and some

Use light tackle, heavy gear is tiring on young arms

appropriate local flies. Heavy gear is a killer for young arms, so avoid it if at all possible.

- To avoid birds' nests in the nylon use only one fly to begin with (i.e. not loch style with droppers) and use a nylon leader no longer than the length of the rod.

- When children are learning to cast keep instructions simple. Something like 'Start low, lift the rod up to your head with a smart flick, pause to let line stretch out behind then cast it toward the horizon' will do. The young are usually far more adept at copying than the older generation. Show them the right way first and then let them get on with it.

- Emphasise keeping bodies balanced and backs reasonably straight. Show them what happens if the rod is dropped too far behind (snags on the bank) or pushed down too hard on the forward cast (brings the line down with a mighty splash). These are the most common beginners' faults.

- Once novices have got the fly out on the water as far as they can, show them an appropriate wet fly retrieve. In the beginning make the novice retrieve with medium pace otherwise they never get the right idea about giving the fly some life in the water. Make them bring the fly to about a rod's length away, lift off and cast out again over a different spot.

- If fishing for wild trout you must always try and cover new ground. Tell the young tyros not to spend too long at one spot. Wild trout are territorial rather than shoaling fish and you must seek them out, they will not swim past you.

- Take breaks between your angling (this applies to adults as well as children!), long periods of apparently casting at nothing is soul destroying. Use these breaks to change the fly, have a snack and/or walk round to a different part of the water.

- Impress that if a trout takes the fly they should 'feel' a pull on the line one way and simply lift the rod tip towards their head to pull the other. Make sure a firm pressure is kept on the fish by holding the rod up, do not let things go slack or the fish might come off.

- Make sure when striking a fish they always lift the rod vertically, pulling it to the side only pulls the fly away from the fishes' jaws. Emphasise it is not always necessary to 'strike' violently, simply meet the fish with equal force to set the fly.

- If wading is allowed and safe on the water you are fishing, show them they can get extra distance when casting by paddling out a little way to welly height. You should encourage them always to start casting near the bank first and then wade gently in – sometimes trout lie close in and too much disturbance should be avoided.

130

- If you and/or your charges have difficulty catching trout remember it could be any one of three reasons. The weather conditions may be unsuitable, you might not be covering enough new trout territories (standing too long in the one spot) or casting styles may be too fish scaring. If you think they are doing everything correctly bar catching fish it could be a change of tactics is required.

- If you are fishing wet fly and then see fish rising on the surface (rings, splashes etc) try using a dry fly such as a dry Sedge, Wickham's, Greenwell's Glory etc. Show the children the difference in the style of fishing but keep the theory brief.

- Teach your children flexibility right from the word go. For example if they do not have specific dry patterns you can always make say a Kate McLaren 'dry' by smearing it with floatant, this will work just as well if the trout are taking insects off the surface.

Teach children to be flexible in their fishing tactics from the start

- Alternatively if you cannot see trout moving at all, try using weighted nymphs on the point fly to take the leader down further or, if casting skills are reasonable, use an intermediate line for depth.

- Remember with intermediate line angling that the line must be rolled to the surface before casting out again. This can be tiring on the arms especially for small children, so only use 'intermediates' with caution and not for too long.

- Encourage children to learn from both their successes and their failures, fishing is a big learning curve and a few disasters along the way are necessary to achieve a balanced perspective.

Disasters happen to everyone!

TROUTFISHER'S TOP TIPS FOR THE SUCCESSFUL INDUCTION OF YOUNGSTERS

1   Above all make the trout angling enjoyable. Fishing is fun, it is a big adventure, a challenge and a game of chance all rolled into one.

2   Children want to be fishing not listening, keep explanations brief and let them get on with it as you stay by their side.

3   Youngsters have many years of the sport ahead of them, just convey your own enthusiasm and your willingness both to help and to listen, then let them learn gradually.

4   Keep a sense of humour and perspective and your patience should be rewarded with a lifelong angling companion.

Part 2

A great place to learn about fly fishing

11

SMALL STREAM/BURN TROUT ANGLING

'The water was very smooth, and there was a feeling of repose and remoteness about it as though it belonged to some enchanted garden and the fairies would come to bathe in it at sundown'
Harry Plunket Greene

THE ATTRACTION

Stream or burn fishing provides a wonderful learning ground, trout fishing in miniature by any other name. This is very much how I and many like minded fisher folk began our fishing careers. Small stream angling is highly suited as an introduction for youngsters new to the sport. There is nothing quite like fishing in a flowing water Lilliput. It is an environment which enriches your angling knowledge and sharpens your reflexes. This kind of angling is always an intimate experience with all your sport taking place within the confines of a concentrated trout habitat. Sometimes you will hit a cluster of determined, hard fighting small trout but equally you can strike nothing. To fish the small stream requires more skill than you might think as casting and landing a fly over the nose of tucked away trout can be an unpredictable business. It is always a challenge but at least it is not normally an expensive one. This angling is often considerably cheaper than trying to fish expensive 'salmon' rivers for trout and having to pay inflated prices for access to fish on particular beats.

It is difficult to beat the uniquely hypnotic rush and gurgle of a sparkling stream as it twists and turns down a hillside or meanders through a valley to meet its inevitable destination. Sometimes it will join a larger lower river sometimes it will end up tipping its contents straight into the sea. Around each bend a new micro environment appears with new features in intriguing diminutive scale to delight the roving angler. Here you will encounter all the features of the big river such as pots, back eddies, riffles, runs, pools and glides all scaled down to miniature size. A river *en petite* it might be but it is a great wild trout fishing environment no matter what you call it.

THE TROUT

Burn/small stream trout are normally beautifully speckled small fish with red

135

and black spots in abundance. Usually they have dark or olive green backs and golden creamy flanks. Little they may be but they are fierce competitors and provide great sport on light tackle. It is interesting that these types of trout can sometimes be unadulterated strains left alone since the last Ice Age. This is especially true if you catch them on stretches above impassable waterfalls where any trout going over cannot return and any incoming trout cannot reach. The Victorians and Edwardians were rampant restocking devotees but they often thought that burn/stream trout were a pest to be ignored in favour of migratory fish. This meant restocking practices were not carried out as much on small streams where the salmon went to spawn and some undiluted strains of trout still exist especially in remote wilderness areas. One thing to beware of is the catching of salmon parr which are clearly recognisable by the grey fingerprint markings along their lower flank. These must be returned gently unharmed and for this reason I suggest using barbless hooks and releasing the little fish under-water if you can.

Trout from the stream

Though burn trout might give the appearance of being babies, some trout will actually be mature fully grown fish maybe seven or more years of age! A really good one might be ¾lb but 6oz to 8oz ounces is much more the norm for these fish. Do not let this put you off however as burn/stream trout offer a realistic and unsentimental idea of what wild fishing is all about. If you begin your angling in stocked 'put and take' fisheries where tame trout are regularly added in at 3lb plus, then you are likely always to want and expect this size of fish. If on the other hand you want to learn about classic angling and remain a wild trout devotee, probably for a lifetime, then stream/burn trouting gives you the 'real thing' in all its glory. Catch these shy spunky fish in their unique territory and you will develop life-long angling skills and be ready to have a go at anything.

TYPES OF STREAM

Broadly speaking the streams of the UK divide themselves into upland and lowland waters.

Upland streams usually descend a steeper gradient than those in low lying areas. The oxygen content in the water will be higher as the current will be faster however the degree of weed growth and invertebrate life is much less. Most upland water courses have pure unpolluted water often of an acidic nature, however the overall fertility can be less than in lowland streams. As a consequence of the generally harsher environment the variety of amount of trout food is reduced and the menu for the resident trout here is more restricted. To cope with this the trout have adapted their growth rates accordingly and will only grow to a size their location can sustain.

Lowland streams usually flow over a more gentle gradient, the current is slower and more meandering and the weed growth is far more sustained and lush. With higher water fertility the diet of the resident trout is greatly enhanced and even very narrow water courses can hold excellent feeding and consequently some fat well-fed trout may linger there. That is the plus side, the minus is the fact that streams in lowland areas often flow through far more populated landscapes and they are therefore likely to be more affected by pollution from industry and agriculture. Because of the slower current, loss of oxygen content in the water from over enrichment by fertiliser phosphates and sewage leeching can be a major problem. It is 'swings and roundabouts' on lowland streams, what you gain in fish size can be destroyed by thoughtless over development.

'In between' streams Note that 'in between' streams is a catch-all term covering streams in different parts of the UK. Remember what Scots may class as a burn, might be classed in England as a full sized river. These national differences must be taken into consideration as they can sometimes be confusing for the visitor. 'In between' streams provide exciting varied fishing from source to estuary beginning as a tumbling upland race and ending as a lowland stream meandering across a valley floor. Numerous 'in between' streams exist in the UK though remember not all parts of them will be fishable as a number of different landowners will come into play. However there is usually enough to keep the ardent small stream fisher happy.

TACKLING UP

The essential factor to consider when selecting equipment for small stream angling is weight. You must fish light and travel light. This means you can leave all those inessential items at home and kit yourself out with suitably minimalist gear. For those used to carting crates of tackle perhaps in the form of different jackets for changing conditions, lines which sink at different weights, landing nets, rods for different waters and/or a selection of waders which reach the thigh, waist or chest, small stream fishing will come as something of a shock. I list below the really necessary items, you can add more if you must but be warned it all gets heavier the further you walk!

Tackle essentials

Light carbon fibre tip to middle action 8ft rod (8ft is a happy 'average' length for small flowing waters), matching lightweight metal reel with a reasonable sized drum to stop kinking in the line and a double taper floating line in the 4/6 DT weight range. Nylon will be non glitter 3lb/4lbBS and it is not normally necessary to take more than one fly box containing river wet flies, nymphs and a goodly number of dry flies all in sizes 14 to 18. To travel light I will wear wellies (you rarely need to

Travel light

wade a small stream unless it is to cross over it), a fishing vest with a light waterproof stuffed in the back 'poacher's pocket' and have all other accoutrements about my person. This will include in no particular order, dry fly floatant and wet fly sink, snips, a hat and sunglasses, midge repellent (essential for Scottish Highlands), food and water and a fish bass to bring back a couple of worthy trout home for the pot if I am very lucky! I don't bother with a landing net especially if the walk is long, as it adds extra weight and I just slip back the wee ones in any case. As long as you have these comparatively few essentials with you, the challenge of burn fishing can be met head on.

TACTICS

The Recce

A good prior assessment of the likely fish-holding spots is essential when you are small stream angling (see also Chapter 7). Look out in particular for places which provide the trout with food traps, shelter from predators and a good flow of oxygenated water. This will mean locating small pools, runnels, areas of light and shade, any overhanging banks, streamy runs, sudden bends, little pots behind boulders in the stream and any back eddies where the water swirls upstream. Fish all likely looking spots carefully for you never know what might be lurking there. The clarity of the water will also give you some indication of the 'spookability' of the resident trout. Gin clear and it is going to be careful stalking and/or casting into riffles rather than glassy glides. Darker water with a hint of peat may mean your intentions are slightly less obvious though you cannot always bank on it!

The conditions on the day should make you decide what tactics you wish to use. I am a great believer in quite literally going with the flow. If it is high water I will often fish downstream wets, with low water it is upstream dries. The wind direction will however dictate the final course of action. Trying to battle upstream with a light line and featherweight dry fly is hard frustrating work if the wind is blasting downstream at a Force 6 or more. Be sensible about things as this kind of fishing is delicacy rather than power.

Concealment

More than anything the key to success in small stream angling is concealment. Burn trout may be eager to feed on your apparently attractive offering of food (the fly) but they also have well developed instincts of self preservation and a great dark object suddenly appearing above their usually open patch of sky is likely to send them running for cover. Remember their environment is tiny compared to ours and to a trout in a diminutive world you will seem like an invading black giant waving a log and a piece of rope! Come to think of it, this is probably why with a little practise, young children can excel at this kind of fishing. Childrens' profiles are that much smaller and they fit that bit easier into the trout's normal field of vision.

For an adult angler to be successful therefore, you must keep back from the water's edge and merge into the lines of the bank as much as is humanly possible. Keep low and as inconspicuous as you can.

Early Season Approach on Small Streams (March to May)

Though trout feeding responses will depend on the nature of the surrounding landscape, it stands to reason that all stream trout will be having a harder time of it during the first half of the season. The water will be colder, higher and faster, food items will be scarcer and trout are sometimes slow to recondition after the rigours of spawning. Consequently the fish may be lying very close to the bank tucked away from the fiercer winter flow of water and concentrating their feeding on bottom crustaceans, molluscs, caddis and any available nymphs. Stonefly nymphs are popular with the trout in March and April as these meaty beasts (which resemble a small scorpion under a magnifier) provide a good sized morsel of protein. Depending on the locale, Large Dark Olives, Stoneflies, Olive Upright, February Red, Yellow Sallies and March Browns may begin to hatch early on. Note these hatches will vary in quantity according to

139

the different upland and lowland stream habitats and in some cases may not be present at all. Also the timing of these hatches may vary though you can usually be guaranteed some action during the warmest part of the day around 1.30pm.

At this time of year your tactics are mainly sub surface and fishing single artificial nymphs like the Sawyer's Pheasant Tail or the Hare's Ear (size 14/16) is usually effective. Heavy nymphs such as those Czech 'Bugs' can also be used though be warned the flow of these smaller waters may not be much and you might find yourself firmly attached to the bottom more than you are able to trundle the nymph in a life-like way. Wet flies such as the Partridge and Orange, Red Tag and the Greenwell's will also be effective and if the day is warm try a small dry Greenwell's, even early in the year the trout can be eager to rise to the floating fly.

Use short lengths of nylon not longer than your rod and a single fly, two if you dare but remember this is small stream fishing and things always seem to snag up that much quicker in this type of environment. Change the fly every twenty minutes or so until you find one the trout will really connect on. Cast a short floating line across and work the nymph/wet fly down in a life-like way so that it reaches into all the little nooks and crannies at the edge of the burn. Do not lift off too fast, each cast must be fished out as often you will find the trout take just as the line is dangling directly downstream close in near the bank. In order to stay concealed a degree of arm extension is involved to work the fly properly. Raise the rod tip, follow the fly down and keep as much of the line off the water as possible. Remember to stay out of sight as much as you can though early on with less intensity of light, you can allow yourself a little leeway in this technique.

Change the fly every twenty minutes or so until you find success

If a trout does take you must strike firmly but not savagely. With these small spirited trout, too fast and you miss, too slow and they are gone! Don't be surprised if the numbers of early season trout in these waters seem slim, they will tend to migrate up and down the stream in search of shelter and food and therefore what fished well mid season the previous year may not be productive early in the new season. Oddly enough when you do catch early stream trout they are often of larger size than the average for the rest of the year. This is because trout may have come up to their natal streams from another (larger) stream and are still lingering there in order to recover. Unless these trout are in mint condition and some will be as they are immature 'crowd followers' it is kinder to return them and let them be on their way.

Mid to Late Season Stream Trouting (May to September)

Once the weather warms and insect life becomes that much more profuse, it is time to consider the dry fly as much as the wet. Trout will be much more spread out across the stream and will be found in most pools and riffles. If there is little rainfall to top up the flow, the fish will tend to concentrate around the areas of greatest dissolved oxygen in faster flowing stretches of broken water. Natural hatches will now include amongst others most types of olives, sedges, mayfly if they exist in the locale, stonefly and midge. If you can see trout rising (and even if you don't) fish a single dry CDC Midge, an Adams or a Rough Olive (size 14 to 18) with the utmost confidence from May onward again on a short line. Darkish grey/brown CDC flies are supreme takers of trout on small waters whether flowing or still, their fine delicate design makes them ideal for this type of miniature angling. Upstream is the norm again on a short line but go with the wind speed and direction. For most of the summer I fish a dry fly upstream *or* across and down with equal success in the small streams. These wild burn trout are not into exact purism in any shape or form!

With the sun now travelling at its highest arc, hiding your intentions becomes critical, keep yourself back from the water and work the fly on raised rod tip. Extend your arm to keep line off the water as with nymph fishing but lift off just before the 'dangle'. Avoid presenting the line to the fish before the fly by a quick lift off to recast. Remember the neat trick of casting lightly on to the opposite bank and then tweaking the fly gently off so that it falls on to the water surface just like a natural insect. This method is extremely effective but needs a fair degree of practise. Too brisk a cast and you will find your fly stuck fast on the opposite bank! The size of trout will now be the average for the stream, often it is on the diminutive side but so what, you are not here for trophies, you are here to hone skills. Bear in mind though that unusually large trout caught in the latter part of the season upstream on a burn linked to the sea may actually be sea trout which have run up on an earlier spate and chosen to stay there. These trout are no longer silver and look all the world like large brownies. It is only when you gut them that you will find their flesh the reddest of red and their stomachs virtually empty of food. Bear this phenomenon in mind when next you catch an unusually large fish in a tiny burn. Sea trout are scarce in many parts of the UK and it would be kinder to future stocks to put back these large trout if caught in areas where the sea trout are under threat.

Common Questions on Fishing the Small Stream

If the trout are so small in these streams why fish for them at all? In this case size has to be immaterial. You do it for the challenge and for the escape into a tranquil little world where Lilliput-sized trout reign supreme.

Is it necessary to match the hatch exactly? With small stream angling as long as you present the fly in a life-like non scary way you have a good chance of catching. Size of fly is often more critical than its colour. The trout are easily spooked by too large an object suddenly appearing in their mini environment.

No matter how hard I work at concealment the trout seem always to know I'm there – what am I doing wrong? Keeping a low profile is essential and your quest is always considerably helped by dull overcast weather when your shadow is not falling across the water. Choose a dark day if you can, also slow your movements down near the water, sudden unusual flashes of light and shadow never help the proceedings.

When striking why do I keep missing trout? There can be two reasons for this; one the trout may be small precocious salmon parr who suicidally lunge at anything that moves often without taking a firm hold of your fly, and two the mature trout will often follow the fly before taking it as if they are sizing it up. You must allow time for this to happen before striking.

I know there is a good trout behind the rock/under the tree below the overhanging bank (insert appropriate description!) but my cast is always clumsy, how can I get at him? Casting into difficult corners takes practise, you need to adapt and rehearse your casting technique for local situations. There are no hard and fast rules but I often find an upstream cast with either dry fly or wet/nymph and then letting the fly drift down with a raised rod tip to keep as much line free of the water, is better than trying to cast downstream. Each situation will be different but stick at it and adapt your casting technique accordingly.

What's the best time of year to fish the little streams? Almost always it is earlier in the season when trout spark into activity and our intentions are not too obvious. Generally speaking on lowland streams this is from early April to late May and on upland streams it is from late April to late June. Taking into account that some streams will fish well throughout the season while others have only short windows of opportunity, good fishing almost always relates to food availability, cover from predators and oxygen content in the water. Once water levels fall things change and fishing generally becomes more difficult.

TROUTFISHER'S TOP TIPS FOR FISHING FOR TROUT IN SMALL STREAMS

1   Don't have too high an expectation of what you are going to catch. Go with a light step and a light heart and go elsewhere if you want large trout.

2   Small streams are an excellent learning ground for youngsters as the intimacy of the water does not seem to them such a threat, it is fishing brought down to their size. For experienced anglers they provide a skill-honing service.

3   Use barbless hooks and quickly return any salmon parr and also any unusually large trout which you think may be sea trout returned to their spawning stream.

4   Use tackle appropriate to the situation in this case light and minimalist. Take small flies in sizes 14 to 18 and be prepared to adapt your casting according to the terrain.

5   Small stream/burn trout may sometimes be easier to attract than their bigger lake or river dwelling cousins but they are no pushover.

Fishing in Lilliput

12

River Trout Fishing

'Nymphing trout look fairly lively in the water... Their tails may be seen to be working, balancing the fish in the current, and they are said by fishermen to be "on the fin"'
Oliver Kite

THE ATTRACTION

The appeal of the big river is omnipotent. The intimacy of the little stream may be gone but it is replaced by a more powerful presence, one that fills the senses and restores the soul. Sometimes the river will be high and mean with its banks flush and the vegetation brushed aside by an urgent current, sometimes it is gently benign with dappled pools glowing and the flow sings a softer benevolent song. The challenge of fishing a big river with all its variations in water height, colour and rate of flow means that tomorrow is always a new day with new tests to face. Instant success with river trout is rare for in order to fish well you need to familiarise yourself with all the moods of the locale. This will mean fishing the river for at least one season with constant attention to detail. The man who claims he can go to any river and catch trout instantly is either very lucky or not telling the truth!

With extra food and cover available river trout tend to be larger and more mobile than their stream cousins simply because of the extra food and cover available. This type of fishing is therefore likely to appeal to those anglers who need something a degree more taxing. Occasionally you will hit a red letter day and hook up with several large wild trout, more often it is a case of thoughtful contemplation of tactics and adapting according to the changing foibles of the big stream. Physically too you will need to have a degree of fitness as reaching the trout can sometimes call for deep wading and you need to be able to hold your balance in some pretty fierce currents.

THE TROUT

Wild river trout are simply bigger versions of their stream relatives and are normally beautifully marked golden specimens with brown backs and butterball flanks. Their increased size is all down to a better food supply and the larger territories they have in which to establish themselves. They will average anything from a few ounces to 3 or 4lb in weight, it all depends on food availability, the

Success!

degree of angling pressure, the amount of inter fish competition, the ease of access to bolt holes to escape predators and the overall fertility of the terrain through which the river flows. The best type of river is one which has a broad range of fish sizes as this shows a healthy natural spawning giving a good spread of year classes. Rivers with mainly tiny trout or a few very large ones might not be doing as well as they could from an angling standpoint.

There are some interesting bloodlines in many river trout populations. As with the trout of small streams you must consider the degree of gene adulteration which has gone on with restocking. On some rivers (particularly Scottish ones containing a strong salmon population) restocking of brown trout will not have been encouraged and original strains will be relatively pure. However on UK rivers where local demand for trout angling may be high, the resident trout can be mainly introduced stockies either the 'put and take' version or fish which have interbred with the original native trout. It is important to remember that some of the best trout chalkstream habitat contains stocked brown trout rather than wild or native fish, all is not quite as it seems!

The degree of trout/sea trout/salmon hybridisation that has occurred due to close proximity of natural spawning redds must also be taken into account. During spawning time intermingling of trout eggs with salmon milt or trout milt with salmon/sea trout eggs is much more common than is supposed. A good example of this is the River Tweed which has one of the highest rates of salmon/trout hybrids in Europe. Here brown trout have a twenty percent salmon

Beautifully marked river trout

gene and this predisposes them to highly dynamic migratory tendencies. Inter-relationships like this with salmon and trout accidentally spawning hybrid offspring are often ignored completely when it comes to conservation of brown trout. In Scotland migratory salmon are covered by one set of laws and non migratory trout by other far less effective ones.

TYPES OF RIVERS

The southern 'chalkstream' river This type of river is characterised by clear, slow pools often in a series of gentle curves which will meander gently across a valley floor until the river meets its final destination. The surrounding environment is likely to be of green fields, water meadows, trees and lush land and aquatic vegetation. The water is normally sweetly alkaline and fertile with good weed growth notably Ranaculus. The river base will be chalk, gravel, clay and rock and the natural feeding for the trout is extensive and rich with an excellent range of insect life and considerable amounts of shrimp, snail and caddis. These rivers are less prone to spates induced by heavy rain as the flow is usually reasonably constant with the water coming from underground aquifers rather than being rainfall led. In the south of England these waters will be known as 'chalkstreams' the Test and the Itchen are classic examples, however it's a mistake to assume a lime-rich environment with prolific feeding for trout can only exist in hallowed southern climes like Hampshire or Berkshire. A number of rivers in the Pennines, Gloucestershire and Derbyshire are rich and lush as are Scottish rivers like the Don, the Lyon and the Tweed. All have equally fertile settings with mineral-rich rocks, increasing the productivity of the water quite dramatically.

Sadly despite these types of river representing some of the most lovely and most photographed countryside in the UK, a few have fallen foul of so called progress. Hefty doses of powerful fertilisers spread on surrounding agricultural land have caused excessive choking algae growth and calamitous over enrichment. Equally, over zealous water abstraction whereby water is removed from the underground reservoirs (aquifers) on the chalk downs for local human consumption, not to mention the ills of industrial pollution, have all helped to nullify some of the finest rivers in the land. The waters still exist but sadly some may have lost a deal of their pristine former glory and may have been turned into stocked 'put and takes'.

The northern 'freestone' river These rivers are almost always fast flowing with more rocky surroundings and are normally situated in the more northern half of the UK above where the land changes from chalky rock to mixes of sandstone, limestone and shale. They have a more urgent flow which tumbles and rushes to its ultimate *dénouement*. Freestone rivers can be more prone to spates being mainly rain fed rather than from aquifers. The weed growth is still reasonable but the character of the river base is more of gravel and different types of rock and less of clay and chalk. Do not let this put you off however for these streams can sustain excellent populations of wild trout. There may be more emphasis on stonefly and midge feeding and less on mayfly but the trout's diet is still pretty good. Freestone rivers are noted for their excellent oxygen content and goodly

River Tweed

concentration of mineral salts, including dissolved limestone in certain areas, and they provide excellent trout habitat. The pH of the water will vary from neutral to slightly acidic and trout grow to surprisingly good weights even in areas of open moorland if the food availability and cover from predators is good. Even if the water is acidic in nature it can be enriched by agricultural run off and trout in lower stretches can reach weights of 3lb plus with 1lb plus the common average.

These types of stream often contain salmon and sea trout as well as browns and you should be aware that your trout fishing can sometimes be limited or made more costly because of the presence of migratory fish. That said there is usually some angling available somewhere, although salmon anglers will often keep quiet about the presence of good sized trout on their waters! You may need to hunt around a bit more for it, but it is there. Be aware of the fact that because the flow in these rivers is prone to sudden spates in times of heavy rain, the river can dramatically colour up with suspended silt and other debris as it scours itself out in a natural but temporarily destructive way. This can disrupt your fishing in dramatic fashion though thankfully the water level usually goes down as quickly as it went up.

TACKLING UP

'The bigger the river the bigger the rod' might be a good maxim but bear in mind this refers more to water height than the actual dimensions of the stream. Nevertheless it is best to face the river with the right level of gear. From experience I would still suggest travelling reasonably light as you will often have long walks to the next suitable trout stretch. This is especially true on rivers also containing migratory fish where trout anglers must give way to salmon anglers particularly on the deep slow pools.

The bigger the river the bigger the rod

Tackle essentials

Normally a light carbon fibre tip to middle action 10ft rod capable of throwing a reasonable length and weight of line is necessary – 10ft is a good multi purpose rod suited to most rivers. When the water height is low you can get by with a 9ft trout rod of similar action. Use a large arbour lightweight metal reel and a selection of lines from sinking to sink tip and from intermediate to floating. Lines should be weighted for the rod but 6 or 7DT or WF are popular choices. Only use a full sinking line if you are up to hauling it up from the depths to recast it as this can be strenuous work in high water. Nylon should be 4lb to 6lb though note some salmon rivers will stipulate a certain density of nylon (4lb or less) so that you do not stay attached to a salmon for very long, perish the thought! Clear nylon is probably better than coloured, dark conditions can make tinted nylon look like a plank of wood to a small fish, think about that time honoured saying 'dark fly for a dark day' if you doubt this theory. A small landing net which can be clipped at your back or side is useful if you are wading. Trout can be beached but you do create a bit of a disturbance wading in and out.

Some anglers will favour tapered or braided leaders which they say are easier to work with in fast water. Good quality tapered leaders give a smoother lift off while some braided leaders are designed to sink and can be useful to attach to your floating line. They then allow you to fish different depths without the added effort of changing to a less easily cast sinking line. If you prefer these, use quality ones otherwise they have a tendency to corkscrew after storage on the reel. Your fly box should contain those flies listed in Chapter 8 in the dry, wet and nymph versions in sizes 14 to 18. You can go smaller down to a size 22 but personally I cannot see well enough to thread the nylon through the eye of this size of hook.

Thigh waders are normally fairly essential on big rivers even if you only stand in water to knee height. Make sure these are studded, big rivers are dangerously slippery places and sadly drownings occur more regularly than they should. If you are using chest waders and again some rivers will not allow this either for conservation or safety reasons, then go with equal care. Unless the sun happens to split the sky you will need a good quality waterproof wading jacket as big rivers can be exposed wet and windy places especially early season. Also have your fishing vest equipped with all the usual items like snips, floatant, sunglasses, food and water and so on. Keep things portable but sensible for the prevailing conditions. If any deep wading is called for you must wear your flotation vest and help yourself stay upright with the aid of a wading stick – be safe at all times, rivers are cold and deadly places to fall into even if you are a good swimmer.

TACTICS

The Recce

This is a vital exercise and to do it successfully you must view the river in both low and high water. The river will have defined fast and slow flowing areas and specific regions where trout will linger in order to have easy access to food and shelter. Such hot spots are not always distinct when the river is high. Though the salmon angler will scoff and stamp an angry foot in times of low water, trout anglers should look upon this time as a highly useful learning experience. It is all very well reading about the fact that trout lie behind boulders, under over-hanging banks, in the lee of bridges, at junctions with incoming feeder streams, in pots and eddies and so on but if you have never established exactly where these features are, you will be fishing semi blind when the river is full.

Take a look at the water clarity, obviously the clearer it is the more you will have to conceal your intentions and creep up on the fish. Chalkstreams and streams running over a light coloured base are often hardest to fish as your dark intent is more visible to the trout. The best conditions for catching river trout will vary according to the locale but if your day is dull with a light breeze and the water is clear and running at average height, then you are in with a shout.

Concealment

While concealing your intentions to trout may not be quite so necessary on the larger expanses of the river, especially one with trees and tall vegetation along its banks, it is still necessary to employ stealth tactics. You may not stick out on the horizon like a large sore thumb as you would do on the bald upper reaches of an upland stream, but you can still make your presence felt by clumsy wading, too much flashy false casting, and inept presentation. Keep your profile merged in with the bank behind and wear clothes of dark hue.

Try and merge your profile into the banks behind

Early Season Tactics (March to early May)

Fishing for river trout when the odd frost is still nipping the air and most vegetation is still struggling into life is often a demanding business especially if the water is high and super fast when compared to later in the year. However, unless the river current is reaching the point of dangerous spate and/or is so dirty with silt run-off that you cannot see more than six inches down, do not be put off by the apparent demands of early season river trouting. If there is a window in the weather, a benign spring day can produce some fabulous fishing, you've just got to be prepared with the right sort of tackle and be fishing in the right place at the right time!

Concentrate your efforts around the warmest part of the day i.e. between say 11am and 3pm for this is the time trout may stir themselves to meet any hatch. As with their small stream brethren, at this time of year the river trout are liable to be feeding more off the bottom of the stream taking amongst other goodies snails, caddis, crustaceans, nymphs and worms as they are swept along in the fast current. If a hatch does come on it is liable to be Stonefly, Iron Blue, March Brown, Large Dark Olives, Large Brook, Turkey Brown or February Red. Keep your eyes peeled for any emerging insects as the hatch is always short and sweet early on, blink and you may miss it!

Now is the time to wear all that neoprene and Goretex and make use of your flotation vest and wading stick. You are not being wimpy in this, you are being sensible. Though the trout may well be lying quite close in escaping the worst of the flow you will on occasion need to get yourself a little further out into the current. Most early season work is done with across and down wet fly or nymph fished on a sink tip or intermediate line. You can use a full sinking line if you wish but it is often hard work to control its progress in a fast current. Popular flies like the Pheasant Tail or the Hare's Ear or wet flies like the Snipe and Purple or the Partridge and Orange can be fished with confidence. Specialist techniques whereby you fish a heavy nymph of tungsten (or similar weighty material) upstream on short floating line and let it drift down in front of you with raised rod tip are useful, but it takes nerve to do this in a raging torrent which threatens to sweep you off your feet! Prior knowledge of the main runs and back eddies of the river helps you know just where the trout are likely to be lying and you should trundle your nymph down over any likely spots even when the water seems too high. Trout are likely to be concentrated in good sheltered food collecting areas and hit these and you will almost certainly hit fish.

If an early season surface hatch does manage to sustain itself then you can switch to small dry flies like CDCs, Black Gnats, Adams, dry March Brown or similar, despite chilly conditions these can be very effective during any obvious feeding activity. Go with the flow.

Mid to Late Season Tactics (May to September)

Once late spring early summer is reached the river trout's menu expands considerably and they may become apparently fastidious in their choice of food. Olives, mayfly, sedge and stonefly are all abundant with mayfly probably the most influential of these hatches sending the trout berserk for a period of anything from two weeks to two months in certain areas. Your choice of artificial fly is more critical now as with the lean months of winter past, the trout are adjusted to sitting in their nooks making split-second choices of what to take from thousands of tasty morsels floating past. Thus if your fly is not quite fitting in with the surrounding goodies they will reject it outright. Why bother with something suspicious if there are plenty of other goodies on the go.

Use upstream dry fly now employing any of those patterns mentioned in Chapter 8 along with your own favourites perhaps going down in size according to water height. Lighten up on your sunk/intermediate lines and go for floaters as the strength of the river current lessens and the water height decreases. Keep your casting delicate, your line in control in the flow and your intentions concealed. Though good trout will still be there you may have to adjust your tactics to fish early morning and late at night. Also you may find that early season trout habitats no longer hold fish as the trout will actively migrate to areas of better shade and cover as well as better feeding. Frequently in big rivers the larger trout seem to disappear come June

The Rough Olive is deadly on most trout rivers

and anglers visiting in summer conditions find themselves hard pressed to attract any trout during daytime. Timing your visit becomes more critical and you really have to go in very dull light to be assured of any contact. Upstream nymph can also be tried when in bright conditions when trout are playing hard to get.

Common Questions on River Trout Fishing

I have become quite proficient at sight fishing i.e. spotting rising trout but still find I spook them when trying to get the fly on their nose If you are trying to fish a downstream fly at a rising fish you must make sure the fly and not the line comes first into the trout's field of view. Keep the line well mended and out of sight of the trout. If you are spooking fish when casting upstream try a cast slightly to one side or the other of where the trout has risen. He may be roving slightly in the current snatching up morsels coming into his territory. If all else fails mark the spot in your mind and rest it for a while before having another go.

When I am fishing across stretches of water which are both riffled and smooth I find it difficult to control the line Remember to raise the rod tip whether wet or dry fly fishing upstream or down. You want to keep as much of the line off the water as possible as soon as the line is laid out flat on the surface the current plays all sorts of tricks on it and the fly's progress is altered. Point the rod towards where the fly is and follow its progress with the tip raised.

What's the best time to fish the bigger rivers to be assured of connecting with trout? As a general rule you should fish during the day early and late season and fish towards dawn and dusk in high summer. Water height plays a critical part however as does the amount of light.

I am often daunted by size when first fishing a new river. Just where do I begin? Seek local advice but remember this may or may not be helpful. Some local experts (see Chapter 2) play their cards very close to their chest and may not necessarily want to divulge their best fishing spots. Rather than looking at the river as a daunting whole see it in sections or beats and fish each as a mini environment. Look out for those trout lies and fish them carefully.

Should I retrieve line when river fishing? Anglers who mainly fish stillwater often retrieve their flies at a similar pace when river fishing. This can have the detrimental effect of tweaking the fly away from the waiting trout before he has a go at it. Obviously you must retrieve a little line so as to keep control but it is not a methodical retrieve like stillwater angling.

Visit your river in low water to locate likely trout holds

Sometimes I catch super trout in one particular spot then later in the year I catch nothing there – why is this? We have already seen that trout migrate towards spawning and better feeding (see Chapter 7). Trout populations vary in their mobility and some will travel some distance to secure food. Oxygen is also a vital requirement and in summer it may be necessary for the trout to drop down to different runs and riffles where the flow of oxygenated water is more concentrated.

TROUTFISHER'S TOP TIPS FOR RIVER TROUT FISHING

1   Remember even if the river you fish is not in a designated chalkstream it can still be rich and fertile with excellent feeding.

2   Visit your river in low water and take note of all the little hidey holes trout may have as well as the oxygen rich channels and runnels within the body of the stream. This gives you a head start in high water, forewarned is forearmed.

3   Use tackle appropriate to water height and the time of year and be safe regarding flotation devices and deep wading.

4   Keeping control of the line and in constant touch with your fly is by far the most important aspect of river trout angling. These trout are fast but cautious and are on and off in a second. It is not so much patience as concentration and determination you need with this game.

13

ESTUARY AND SALTWATER TROUT FISHING

'On more than one occasion my suggestion of attempting to fish certain salt water estuaries has been scoffed at by local people, but I have sometimes been surprised at the results'
MacDonald Robertson

THE ATTRACTION

Fishing for trout where freshwater meets salt always has an element of derring do about it. This is risky, unpredictable wild trout fishing taken to extremes. Gone are your familiar landmarks of soft green fields, moors and trees and instead you look largely upon sand, rocks and bladderwrack weed. The constant noise of an unforgiving ocean fills your head as gulls wheel and screech on an endless horizon of wind and wave. Seals and the occasional otter provide some company for the salt water trout fisher but largely you are on your own in an exciting but uncompromising world.

Some freshwater fishers do not rate saltwater angling highly, claiming it has little appeal perhaps because of the threatening vastness of the ocean. I have to admit there is something in this pessimism, especially if you arrive on a dark gale-riven day when great spumes of sea spray hit the rocks like shattered glass. However given a relatively benign spell of weather the prospects are completely different. Those who scoff at this branch of our sport miss out on a considerable amount of joyous and intensely challenging angling. For all its unpredictability, there is still much to commend this branch of the sport. The rewards are considerable with heart-stopping action coming in sudden intense bursts of activity. Tide timetables make estuarine angling less sustained than day long river trout fishing, yet when the trout are taking the glorious 'highs' of this type of angling are far greater in intensity. I urge you to try it.

THE TROUT

With this type of angling the fish you might make contact with are resident river trout, slob trout or migratory sea trout. Basically these are all of the same species, it is just that river trout have made their principal home in freshwater, slob trout have taken up station in the brack (where salt and fresh waters meet)

Uist Estuary – benign in the sun

while sea trout are fish which have undergone a smolt stage and then actively migrated to saltwater to gain access to better feeding. Often the size of the sea going trout is better than the norm due to the extra nutrition the fish take on while in the salt. Sea trout may be anything from 1lb to 5lb plus while slob trout can be of similar proportion. Interestingly the resident freshwater dwelling river trout are often of smaller size and a 1lb fish amongst them might be classed as a very good catch. This is usually because they have not switched to the richer feeding in the salt. I am certain such feeding patterns are down to genetics, the trout with the strongly migratory gene go to sea and fatten up while the others do not leave the confines of the main river.

Despite the obviously intriguing genetic mix of these trout, very little research seems to come to the attention of the angling public. All too often the only time we hear of sea trout studies is when evidence is being sought as to why so many migratory trout populations have crashed, notably on the west coast of Scotland where the blame has been laid squarely on the shoulders of intensive fish farm/aquaculture interests. Sadly even when reports clearly reveal that migratory trout leave their freshwater habitat to cruise up coastal saltwater waters for two years or more *and* that fish farms and all their attendant pollution/sea lice infestation are obviously in the fishes' cruising paths, it is naive to assume that any government might act on such information. It is a fact of angling life that important research like this is often only done when it is too late to help, the history of British angling is littered with cases of trying to shut the stable door after the horse has bolted.

When estuary fishing, many anglers will concentrate their efforts on the migratory sea trout as these offer stupendous sport in the right conditions. Knowledge of the fishes' life cycle helps considerably in the quest. While at sea, shoals of sea trout will cruise up and down relatively nearby coastal waters picking up extra nutrition. At this stage the young fish are known in Scotland as finnock or less commonly as whitling, and while an 'average' size may be a 1lb or so, larger trout up to 5lb are reasonably common amongst the smaller fish. There is sometimes confusion as to how long this oceanic phase can last for though the shoals of trout may return to their natal streams after six months or so, it does not necessarily follow that all sea trout do so. Even when the sea trout return to freshwater they may not all go on to spawn. Some trout seem to take longer to reach maturity and will be 'crowd followers' in both fresh or saltwater. Crowd followers simply seem to go up with the pack but may not be mature enough to reproduce.

Sutherland sea trout – a master of the sea

Once they have run back upstream to completely fresh water the migratory trout begin to lose their silver colouration and return to a more 'brown trout' livery. A spawned sea trout is known as a kelt and these spent fish may return to sea after spawning and then recondition and run upstream again next season. Some misunderstanding exists over kelt trout for though early season fishing can indeed produce a few spent fish which must to be returned to recondition, it does not always follow that all early season sea trout are kelts. Far from it for some trout which have overwintered at sea have not spawned at all and are in excellent mint silver condition. By and large most will be immature finnock sized averaging around about 1lb but some are quite a bit bigger at 3lb plus.

P. D. Malloch observed this way back in 1909 when he wrote of catches of sea trout on the Tay in February which consisted of mint condition sea trout of 1lb 8oz none of which had spawned.

TYPES OF ESTUARINE ENVIRONMENTS

Sand/mud flats estuaries Classical saltwater estuary fishing normally takes place on wide areas of sand and/or mud flats where a river and/or several small streams meet the sea. At high tide these flat sandy areas are often covered by sea water while at low tide the channels of the various freshwater inflows are exposed. This type of environment is ideal for shoals of young sea trout which drift in and out on the tide chasing sand eels, crustaceans, worms and other small fish. On incoming tides the sea trout shoals come in to access the feeding and nose the freshwater inlets, then as the tide recedes the fish drift off and return to deeper water.

Tidal water Some rivers have very little in the way of fiord-like streams and instead may tip their contents straight into the ocean. Rivers where town estuaries have been dredged for industrial uses fall into this classification and fishing these can be daunting as boats race in and out from harbours and jetties. Anglers may be reduced to fishing off piers but if you catch the tide times this can still be very productive even if the species waver between trout, pollack and bass!

TACKLING UP

The vital thing to remember about choosing tackle for salt or brackish water is that it is likely to rust if not washed after use. It makes eminent sense not to take the best rod and reel out on an estuary! Basically you can use the same equipment as for the bigger river with the caveat of stronger nylon.

Tackle essentials

Use an old 10ft to 11ft rod and matching reel (nowadays you can buy reels built to withstand the effects of saltwater), floating or intermediate line with WF7 popular to cope with strong winds, 6lb to 8lb nylon and a selection of traditional sea trout patterns together with streamer flies to imitate sand eels. Fly size needs to err on the bigger than normal, anything from size 6 to 10 is commonly used with size 12s occasionally used in difficult low water conditions. Some form of wading is usually necessary and it is essential to have boots with good studs to avoid slipping on the weedy rocks. A wading stick is useful and as sea trout favour dark, dirty, days it is best to use good quality waterproofs. A small landing net is recommended if you are fishing over a rocky shore and you feel the fish may be lost if you beach it. Good waterproofs and the usual fishing vest with accoutrements should be worn and having a book of local tide timetables helps considerably in planning your time of attack.

TACTICS

The Recce

Knowing the daily time of high tide is critical to success in saltwater trout fishing as all ocean dwelling creatures are influenced by the rise and fall of the tides. Fishing is generally best when the tide is coming in (say two hours prior to high tide) when the waves are pushing the sea trout's staple diet inshore. Shoals of trout follow the sand eels and their presence is given away by leaping fish and also by predatory seals following on behind. Seals are of course an absolute nuisance but their appearance means fish are close by and that it is time for action. On some estuaries which flood quickly and/or unpredictably, the best and safest time to fish has got to be two hours after high tide when the fish have come in and are slowly falling back to sea. Visiting the intended area of fishing at low tide is tactically vital as it allows you to see the channels and runs of fresh water as they cut their way over the sand. Also at low tide you will see the favoured sea trout lies next to weed and rocks possibly with some sand in between. These features are usually where sea trout gain access to food (sand eels and small fish) and shelter from predators.

Concealment

There is often the argument that sea trout are so shy you can only catch them at night when darkness conceals your intentions. While this is partly true you should not forget you can still have success during daylight hours providing the conditions are dull, driech and breezy with the odd shower of rain. Your profile should merge into the banks behind (if there are any) but given a dark gloomy day there is no absolute need to adopt an extremely low stance, in fact it will be impossible to do this if you are stuck miles out on a mud flat.

Visit the fishing area at low tide to recce runs of fresh water

Early Season Tactics (March to May)

Err on the side of caution when early season angling as you may attract a kelt or two but this must not deter you from trying as there are excellent clean non spawning trout always around at this time. Kelts though silvery in colour, have long lank bodies, possibly kyped jaw line and all in all look decidedly out of condition. Put any such catches back for it is the overwintered sea dwelling fish you are after. Fishing two hours before the high tide especially when the moon's phases indicate higher than average tides is usually productive in overcast conditions. Pick your fishy 'food and shelter' targets near rocks, weed and sand and try and cast near where there are freshwater channels running into the sea.

When angling for the sea trout normally you use something like a Teal Blue and Silver as a tail fly and a Blue or Black Zulu top dropper. Red Invicta and Dunkeld are also excellent as are home made hair wing/streamer flies in sand eel colours (olive green, silver and gold). Fish your flies fast across the current/wave action. Sea trout are used to chasing prey and this is the classic method in the brack. Use at least 6lb nylon on intermediate or floater and keep trying around the narrowest part of the channels. Don't worry if it all seems terribly dead, periods of inactivity are common in this type of angling, however once a shoal is on the move it has got to go past you at some point. Draw any captured trout to the side quickly to avoid too much commotion amongst the fish. The action will be brisk and all too quickly past but it is heart pounding when it is on.

Early season is often good for slob trout though be careful you do not take baggots (female sea trout which have not spawned) or kelts. The 'slobs', which I prefer to call big browns as this is a ghastly name for a noble fish, are often lingering in areas of the river where the incoming tide technically stops and the fresh water begins to dominate. A prior recce to ascertain roughly these productive areas helps considerably in planning your line of attack. Though these big trout will take sea trout patterns as already mentioned they can also be caught on smaller river/loch flies both dry and wet. A Butcher's or an Invicta work well sub surface as do small dry sedge patterns or a Rough Olive if the trout are actively rising.

Mid to Late Season Tactics (May to September)

May must be counted as the principal starting time for the salt/brack trout season and it will reach a peak by July slowly dovetailing to late September. Although catches can and are made before May, the weather can be so diabolically unpredictable that the chances of getting a decent day are greatly reduced. Although you are fishing tidal waters in mid season the amount of fresh water in the inflowing streams still plays an important role in your success rate. A wet summer will sometimes mean the sea trout run up river faster and earlier than usual and may not be present for very long in the estuary. Conversely a dry summer means the trout linger longer in salt or brackish areas as they await water levels rising. However be guided by regional advice for the trout of the brack show different behaviour patterns depending on their location. In northern areas like Shetland and Orkney there are sea trout populations which largely remain at sea edging in and out on the tides before the majority finally go upstream in late October or early November to reach the spawning grounds.

The same flies are used as for early season with Teal Blue and Silver the top favourite for many salt and brackish waters. Expect superbly fighting fish but again time your efforts to catch the two hours before the peak of the tide and/or the two hours after according to local custom. With the lengthening hours of daylight, dull overcast days are now essential and you can also fish well into the gloaming if fatigue does not overcome you. Night fishing is also successful for sea trout lingering in the brack, and it is all exciting stuff.

Traditional flies including Zulus, Invictas and TBS – all great for sea trout

Common Questions on Tidal Fishing

With so much coastline where are the best tidal fishing waters in the UK?
Going by reputation the better sea trout fishing lies off Shetland, Orkney, the Outer Hebrides, parts of Ireland and the western coast of Scotland. There is however excellent sea trout fishing on Border rivers such as the Tweed and the Annan and we must not forget the Welsh streams famous for their sewin (sea trout). Good sea trout are caught off the Isle of Man, in fact the list is much longer than you would think. The main prerequisite for good tidal fishing is a strong flushing tide and clean fresh water inflows.

Apart from the obvious threat of bright sunshine putting the fish down are there other weather factors affecting the catching of sea/brack dwelling trout?
The wind is a key factor in estuarine fishing. If you have prolonged strong onshore winds, clouds of silt and sand tend to pile up at the stream/river mouth and fish are sometimes disinclined to venture closer in. Catches are therefore often affected.

Is it still possible to catch trout at dead low tide? When the tide is well out, fishing is often less productive than during a moving tide. However if you have no choice but to fish when the tide is dead low seek the slob/river trout first as they are often more obliging. Some tidal movements take the sea trout well out to sea and you cannot reach them. Seek local advice however as different areas fish in different ways.

I have followed the tide times religiously but still catch very little, why? It could well be you are not fishing at the right time of year and/or you are in an area damaged by fish farming interests. The movements of sea trout are uncommonly difficult to track and some years they are simply not there in such great numbers. Regarding fish farms, these ugly blots on the landscape are highly visible and it is best not to fish near them unless you want to catch trout with heavy sea lice infestation or none at all!

I have tried the time honoured across and down technique letting the fly swing round slowly in the current but never seem to attract much other than small resident browns, why? Sea trout need something to chase and a slow drift down does not normally work for the larger predatory fish straight from the sea. Personally the only time I find a straightforward across and down works well is when the current of the inflowing river is very fast, normally a quick retrieve of the flies is needed for success.

TROUTFISHER'S TOP TIPS FOR SALTWATER/ TIDAL TROUT FISHING

1   Do not be put off by locals proclaiming that saltwater trout angling is rubbish. This happens a lot (even when the angling is good!) so make the judgement for yourself. Does it look a good fishy spot with plenty of sandy bays, a good clean inflowing stream and/or river, plenty of bladderwrack weed, rocky outcrops, seals visible and no aquaculture nearby? If the answer is yes then you have nothing to lose in having a go especially on an incoming tide.

2   Beware of catching kelt trout early in the season but do not let this stop you from at least having a few casts. Sometimes you can be pleasantly surprised with some fine sea wintered fish.

3   Wash all tackle in freshwater when you are finished otherwise when you next use it, rust and grit will have won the day!

The Kyle – a hairwing variant for sea trout

14

SMALL STILLWATERS

'There is no doubt that the angler will always fish best when he employs methods in which he has most confidence'
R. C. Bridgett

THE ATTRACTION

Of all the forms of trout angling undertaken in the UK, bank fishing on small inland waters is almost certainly the most popular in terms of numbers participating. Stillwaters of lesser water volume are everywhere in the form of small lakes, ponds, reservoirs, lochans and tarns and most contain a mix of sporting and/or coarse fish. Because of the burgeoning popularity of rainbow trout 'put and take' fisheries you may find small exclusively brown trout stillwaters rather thin on the ground especially near our main cities. However if you are selective there are venues where brown trout are still the main quarry and of course if you are prepared to travel you can enjoy thousands of small 'stillwaters' i.e. wild trout lakes/lochs in the upland regions of Scotland and Wales. Though some small waters will have boats for hire I will deal with boat angling specifically in the chapter on larger stillwaters as I feel boats should principally be used when there is a bigger expanse of water to be covered.

The appeal of small stillwaters lies very much in their relative intimacy, their horizons are not too vast and exposed and you can normally explore most of the shoreline on foot. If you want 'buddy fishing' where you can see your pals' every move then you can do that on many lowland stillwaters, if you want demanding fishing in splendid isolation high in the hills that too is very easily obtained. While trout stream/river fishing in certain areas may be hard to come by, either because of expense or because salmon angling prevails, there will nearly always be some kind of stillwater trout angling available close to our main centres of population. Undoubtedly many of these waters will have been stocked either in the past or as on-going practice, however they still offer the improver a fine challenge as well as being an ideal learning ground for the novice.

THE TROUT

Leaving aside rainbow trout, the quarry we are hoping to catch in small stillwaters will range from some reasonably genetically pure native brown trout to one hundred percent farm raised stockie browns. Today the majority of trout populations

The appeal of small stillwaters lies in their intimacy

in most small UK stillwaters are composed of generations of stocked browns which have gone on to spawn naturally in the wild. Because of the popularity of this form of trout fishing, numerous stillwaters have been stocked since the early 1800s in order to provide sport and recreation. Indeed in Victorian times most lakes/lochs with towns or villages nearby saw some form of restocking whether they actually needed more trout or not. If the water concerned had reasonable natural spawning facilities then generations of stocked and native fish bred together. With plenty of stocked trout available to top up constantly the water and keep anglers happy, new stock additions may not seem terribly important. However native trout carry the genes for survival in specific habitats, they are the wolves of the water, newly added stew pond trout are but the poodles! We should always ask ourselves what we want to catch and take it from there.

The natural feeding in small stillwaters can often be better than in rivers especially if local streams are fiercely fast flowing with high acidity. Waters without heavy currents can provide a less stressful environment for the trout and if the competition for food is not too intense in the stillwater then the trout will grow to a fair size. Anything from say ½b to 2lb plus can be expected in an average brownie stillwater with larger sizes present if the water is particularly fertile. The best waters

from an angling point of view, are ones with a good cross section of fish sizes preferably of naturally spawned brown trout. Even though the original strains of trout may be diluted or indeed non existent the fish are usually of excellent quality and you should not be deterred from enjoying this kind of fishing. These environments provide important retreats from the extraordinary world we now live in.

TYPES OF SMALL STILLWATER

Minor lowland stillwaters In this class we see small reservoirs, ponds, lakes and small low-lying lochans. These waters may be naturally formed or partly man made with the controlling addition of dams usually for water supplies. In general terms the feeding in lowland waters is usually richer than in their highland counterparts, waters are often spring fed, shallow and lush. Plant growth is usually more substantial and provides good shelter for the fish. Banks will be agricultural or tree lined to a certain degree and shorelines can be any combination of clay, mud, gravel and rock. Generally the trout have a less harsh existence than in upland waters however there are some disadvantages to this type of environment. These include fluctuations in water height especially if it is being used as a reservoir – remember as soon as the margins dry out the trouts' food supply decreases. Also the fact that in times of hot weather small sheltered stillwaters can be very prone to deoxygenating algae blooms which in some cases are toxic to humans and fish.

Small upland stillwaters In this class are highland hill lochs and upland lakes and tarns. Most are naturally formed waters fed from springs and rainwater run off. Normally the feeding is less rich than in lowland waters but remember the limestone-bearing rocks of the far north and the mineral enriched waters of Northern England. Though altitude is an influence (food chains flourish later than in the lowlands) it is not a critical one, the base of the stillwater and the surrounding landscape are still the most important factors in determining fertility. The banks are more likely to be open moorland, heather and rough grazing and the base normally a combination of different rocks, sand and/or peat. Plant growth in these waters may be less profuse or it may be the same as lowland waters but commencing its growth cycle a little later. These waters can be less prone to algae blooms because of their more exposed positions and buffeting by high winds, however there are exceptions to this rule notably in Shetland where amazing blooms occur on a few remotely situated lochs in May when sunshine hours first lengthen. Oxygen content is likely to be naturally higher but acidity in upland stillwaters may sometimes be greater especially if the water is surrounded by peat.

TACKLING UP

Choice of tackle depends very much on whether you are fishing a lowland water

Small upland waters – travel light

with user friendly facilities like car parks, toilets and lunch hut or whether you are heading for the hills where there are little or no such creature comforts. Tackle should suit the venue. If you are choosing an easily accessible water then you can afford the luxury of extra jerseys, jackets and boots stashed in the car in case the weather changes. However if your choice is the high tarns then you must go suitably equipped with gear you can physically carry all day.

Tackle Essentials

Whether you are on high or low ground a functional 9ft to 10ft light carbon fibre rod, matching reel and a selection of floating, sink tip and intermediate lines (weights 5 to 7WF or DT) should do the trick. Nylon should normally be 4lbBS, some may use fine 3lb tippets but my preference is for something that will hold that big 'un (ever the optimist!). Tapered leaders can be used if the water is very clear and fish seem easily spooked however I often use a length of clear non glitter nylon which puts the biggest fine tippet distance between the end of the fly line and the fly itself. Note tapered leaders are useless if you are going to fish droppers as you end up trying to put droppers on the thicker parts of the nylon and the whole thing becomes unbalanced. The fly box should contain a goodly selection of the stillwater flies mentioned in Chapter 8 in wet, dry and nymph mode. Sizes of fly for little inland waters may be correspondingly reduced say from 12 down to 16 but a lot depends on the conditions when you arrive. Some small stillwaters might require wading but most can be fished directly from the bank and wellies are often sufficient, this applies to upland and lowland venues. In addition if you have a long walk ahead, wellies are the only option, wearing neoprene 'chesties' to climb hills is asking for major trouble, heat exhaustion and/or dehydration are often the result. A small landing net may ease landing fish though if you are angling on high hill lochs leave it behind and beach or release fish, it is too much to carry.

Whatever your altitude carry your essential accoutrements of snips, floatant, sunglasses etc in your fishing vest and try and travel light, fatigue from being overburdened decreases your fishing abilities considerably. If heading into a remote area take a rucksack rather than an over the shoulder tackle bag as this spreads the weight much better across your back. Make sure you pack a relevant map and compass, plenty of food and water, a space blanket in case you are benighted, whistle, torch and spare fleece. Waterproofs should be light and of good quality whether you are up hill or down dell.

A fishing vest is indispensable

TACTICS

The Recce

Despite the fact that, in the case of lowland water, many anglers may have tramped the banks before you, the recce is still essential before you start. For the hill loch explorer it's equally important – forget any notion that just because your selected remote water is infrequently fished the trout will throw themselves at you – such occurrences are all too rare. When you first look at an unfamiliar small stillwater it can all appear fairly uniform in character. Your job will be to suss out features which break up this homogeny like islands, promontories, skerries, weed beds, underwater reefs, shelves, drop offs, bays, fences, inflowing streams and any overhanging vegetation which extends over the water surface. Concentrate your efforts around these first. Like river browns, the trout of stillwater will each have relatively defined territories with the best provinces i.e. those with easiest access to food and shelter, dominated by the biggest fish. Land features which cause wind currents to trap food and provide a degree of refuge for trout are popular 'hot spots' as are aquatic features such as weed beds.

Concealment

If the day is calm and bright and the water gin clear, you could be in for a tough time on your favourite small water. Concealment becomes paramount to success and you should use a low profile and clothing of dull hue. Blend yourself in with the bank as much as you can and before you fish glance over your shoulder at what is behind. If there are trees, high banks or thick vegetation your casting may need to be accurate but your outline will not be so noticeable to the fish. This can give you a head start on the anglers who are atop bald banks or out on high promontories. If conditions are dull and overcast then concealment, while still important, is not such a big issue. I wade a number of local small lochans where the trout will rise almost beside me providing that it is a dark breezy day.

167

Early Season Tactics (March to May)

Brown trout which have spawned in October and November can be in good condition right from 15 March especially if the bottom feeding is rich and the fish have enjoyed a mild winter. Kelt brown trout do occur, they look lean and dull with floppy bellies but they are in the minority, if you encounter a poor looking specimen (often it is a bigger than normal trout) then return it to fatten up for later on. In general trout will be hugging the margins just now as they try and recover after the rigours of overwintering. They are also close to the edge to seek shelter away from rough weather. Sadly in our eagerness to cast a long line we often forget this early season fact and 'line' (spook) many more trout than we actually catch.

Now is the time for traditional flies such as the Soldier Palmer, Kate McLaren or Black Zulu. Invictas are also exceptionally useful point flies. I bank fish a team of two flies now with a medium paced 'loch style' retrieve with a light dibble of the top dropper before lift off. Normally most takes come to the sunk point rather than the bob/top dropper fly. Unless the water is exceptionally deep close in I will still use my floating line early on working on the principal that the trout are near the edges anyway. As with early season angling on flowing water you have to concentrate your efforts around the warmer parts of the day, normally between 11am and 3pm with a peak about 1.30pm. 'Always have your fly in the water at half past one' is a good old saying and one particularly applicable to this type of early angling. A team of nymphs like GRHE and Cove's Pheasant Tail are also good now fished slowly either on a long leader and floating line or on an intermediate.

When bank fishing cast across the wind for better fly presentation

When bank fishing small stillwaters your method is usually a cast out across the wind if you can as this gives a better presentation of your flies. If the wind is too strong however then you will have to fish with it at your back. Once you have got the fly/flies out on the water keep your rod tip parallel with the surface as you retrieve and cast and walk rather than standing still. You must hunt out those fish for unlike rainbows they are not going to swim past you. Try and cover a new sector of water each time you cast and keep moving until you find trout. Around the top of the day (1.30pm) there will often be a hatch of midge, pond olive and/or stonefly especially in mid April, and the appearance of an abundant surface food supply after months of bottom feeding often sends the trout into a mini feeding frenzy. It will not last long but make the most of it. A small dry Greenwell's or Brown Sedge is remarkably effective during these brief hatches.

Mid to Late Season Tactics (May to September)

Once we reach mid May the water warms and the first daphnia blooms of the season begin. Trout follow this organic soup as it travels upward during darker hours and downward in bright sunshine. Though the surface hatches of mayfly, sedge, olive, stonefly and midge will also increase in intensity, the appearance of microscopic daphnia marks the first big switch in trout feeding behaviour and gets them into gear for coming events. Imitation of these tiny water fleas is impossible but simple interception of feeding fish is usually sufficient. Bright attractor patterns such as Silver Invicta, Clan Chief, Soldier Palmer or Zulus are all excellent for daphnia-feeding trout.

As the season develops the emphasis is on a wider range of tactics from traditional loch style wets with floating line to sunk nymphs on intermediate line, the latter being used specifically in periods of brilliant sunshine. Dry fly on a floating line does exceptionally well from May and the old trick of a dry fly top dropper and a wet fly on the point is highly productive now if you feel trout are feeding at different depths. With increasing food availability trout will spread out more across the water and can be found both close in and offshore. Even in high summer it still pays to begin your casting close in before lengthening line. Use any or all of the dry/wet/nymph flies recommended in Chapter 8 and go for it.

The best summer stillwater trouting often occurs at either end of the day rather than when the sun is travelling directly overhead. However given a dull windy day you can still enjoy excellent 'top of the day' fishing. Your tactics are similar to those of the early season but you now have the added bonus of casting to rising fish. Keep your eyes and ears pinned back for the sound or sight of a rise, if they are rising they are taking. As soon as a hatch like sedge or olive reaches a certain intensity you will see trout start to rise determinedly (the Abundance Factor) your job now is to get your fly amongst them. Preoccupation with a particular insect can make the trout appear as if they are not interested in your own imitation but stick at it. They are making choices from thousands of hatching insects and providing yours looks and behaves in a similar way, be patient for they will have a go at it in the end. This is a very intense kind of fishing but to me it is the most rewarding. If dry fly is apparently not working a useful tactic is to try a sunk wet of similar hue to the hatching insect. | 169

Common Questions on Fishing Small Stillwaters

I spend lots of time on the bank casting over favoured hot spots yet catch little, why? The answer to this could be anything from clumsy casting to the wrong choice of flies but, assuming a reasonable skill level, the usual answer to this is you are spending too long in the one spot. Fish as fast as the drifting boat and be a hunter not a statue.

I see lots of people buzzer fishing with a very slow retrieve, should I follow suit? Not necessarily, I often find a size 14/16 dry fly equally effective on small waters, 'buzzer' (small nymph) fishing is a tactic grown out of rainbow trout angling. Sometimes it is useful for browns especially in hard-bright conditions but standard wets or dries are just as good if not better.

Is it impossible to catch trout in brilliant sunshine? No, a lot depends on the wind direction. I made up a saying a while back about this 'When sun and wind align the fishing will be far from fine'. This basically means you can fish in bright sun as long as the bright light is on the trouts' backs rather than shining directly in their eyes.

Does it make a difference to the fishing if the trout are stocked rather than wild fish? When trout are mixed generations of stocked and native fish the end result is normally still of very good quality. If they reproduce naturally in the wild they are technically wild fish. Small stillwaters totally stocked with browns can provide good sport provided the stocking is not overly intensive and the trout have been put in as fingerlings and allowed to mature over a fair period of time.

Hill loch fishing at Scourie

TROUTFISHER'S TOP TIPS FOR FISHING ON SMALL STILLWATERS

1. Be flexible in your approach, even on small waters each day will see something different happening and you should adapt tactics from dry to wet according to conditions.

2. Keep moving on the banks and hunting the trout, they will not come to you.

3. Remember the daphnia trigger as the arrival of these little creatures seems to stimulate trout into feeding mode and put them on the alert for the coming hatches of olive, sedge, mayfly and midge.

4. Trout will feed on the most abundant items prevailing in the food chain, getting to know the timing of your local hatches helps considerably. Absolute imitation is not always crucial, interception of feeding fish will often be enough.

15

LARGE STILLWATERS

'...he hath told me he thought that Trout bit not for hunger but wantoness;
and it is the rather to be believed'
Isaak Walton

THE ATTRACTION

The appeal of big lake/loch fishing lies partly in a sense of freedom to explore and partly in the anticipation of encountering a wider range of trout sizes with possibly a larger than average fish amongst them. Vast sweeping horizons may be slightly daunting to some especially on a wild windy day yet to the adventuring angler there is always one more bay to investigate, always one more headland to fish. Out on the big loch there is space, somewhere to breathe deeply, absorb the immense sky, forget the mundane and of course concentrate on some seriously good fishing.

While some of the big waters may have other species present (coarse fish or

A sense of freedom

rainbows) in the main the resident brown trout will be wild fish which may have seen less in the way of restocking practices. Stock additions to very large sheets of water are an expensive business and therefore native trout in these stillwaters may have seen less strain dilution. If the lake concerned is exceptionally popular with huge numbers of anglers wanting to visit then management policy may well be to restock, however for the most part the brown trout residing in the UK's big lochs/lakes/loughs are indeed the 'real thing'.

THE TROUT

Trout in large stillwaters deserve much more attention than they currently receive. Unseen except by anglers, a glorious range of beautifully marked trout swim in the depths and it is my opinion these fish are the 'true Brits'. They should be nurtured and preserved rather than have their territories invaded by carelessly introduced fish. Though technically they are all simply called *Salmo Trutta* the trout range from what we know as classic wild brownies of a few ounces to a couple of pounds through to the gorgeous Ferox of 6lb to 20lb plus. Localised populations of Lake trout, Sonaghen, Gillaroo, Yellow Bellies, Leven Trout, Grey, Golden and White Trout are also there. Regular fishers of big waters know they can capture trout with certain markings and colouration in particular loch/lakes and that is how those original names came about. It is only comparatively recently however that definitive research by the University of Belfast on Lough Melvin in Ireland proved that different strains of trout complete with their own spawning areas can co-exist in one aquatic habitat. This to me should have acted as a catalyst in propelling research into other unique populations of lake/loch trout with a view to their better conservation, however though this may indeed be happening it is not exactly high profile which is a great pity.

Growth rates of local trout populations in big lochs vary considerably. You would think since there is such a large expanse of water that trout would spread out so that competition for food would be lessened however it seems very much that genetics determine where the trout linger, how fast they grow and how far they roam. Ferox for example have very different lifestyles from ordinary brownies in that they have a sudden dramatic growth spurt from aged three years plus and take to predating on other fish species notably charr. They also hunt much deeper, thirty or forty feet down and this behaviour is radically different from brownies which prefer comparatively shallow water. Although Ferox are an obvious example other trout show different growth rates within a specific water with some remaining forever on the small side until death while others like Yellow Bellies growing to fine eating size (1lb approx) within three to four years. Large stillwaters where there is a healthy cross section of fish sizes always provide the most exciting fishing.

A fine sea trout from Loch Hope, Altnaharra

TYPES OF LARGE STILLWATER

Lowland waters Irish loughs are classic shallow lowland waters with high fertility and a massive amount of fishing space. They are eutrophic waters, limestone enriched and enjoy excellent hatches of most insect life notably mayfly but most things a trout would eat are available in these types of water. Just as with small stillwaters it is what lies at the bottom and around the shores which has the biggest influence on the trout therein. The banks will be a mix of green agriculture and some moorland and everything points to rich shallow waters with fat, well fed trout present. Some larger English waters like Rutland come close in fertility as do various Scottish lochs such as Loch Leven. Despite their northern location the big lochs of Orkney, Loch Spiggie in Shetland and Loch Watten in Caithness also offer classic 'lowland' fishing. The water will normally be spring fed and clear or in moorland dominated areas it may be slightly tea coloured. The shorelines are usually indented and there will be numerous little bays and islands to fish round.

Loch St Johns, a rich eutrophic 'lowland' water of the Far North

Upland/glacial lochs These are much deeper dramatic troughs of water carved out by the movement of glaciers across the UK notably in the Highlands of Scotland. The character of these vast stretches of water is decidedly different with great mountains dwarfing the fishers below. The water will tend to be more acidic with rainwater and peat run off (oligotrophic) with rocky shores and poor weed growth. In this harsher less productive environment, trout growth rates are correspondingly slower. These deep waters may be the main habitat for that mega trout the Ferox but it is normally populations of smaller trout which haunt the margins. Many glacial lochs have been altered in nature by the introduction of dams for hydro-electric power however the trout fishing is normally still good providing you are selective in picking your drift and keep to the most fruitful areas.

TACKLING UP

Big expanses of water call for the big guns in terms of tackle but for rods that does not mean heavier but longer. You need to be able to cast and work flies all day often sitting down in a boat and if you are using too weighty an ensemble, fatigue sets in and mistakes will be made. Comfort should be your main priority.

Tackle Essentials

To all intents and purposes big stillwaters cry out for 'loch style' gear and a 10ft to 11ft rod is usually used along with a matching large arbor reel, floating inter-mediate and sinking lines (WF7 is the most used popular) and nylon 4lb to 6lb. Classic wet, dry and nymph patterns should litter your fly box in size 10 to 12 with a few 14s for difficult days. Whether you are boat or bank angling you are going to need wellies or thigh waders if only to get you in and out of the boat and keep your feet dry. Likewise you will need your indispensable fishing vest with your usual accoutrements: sunglasses, snips, floatant, spare spools etc. A hot drink is always welcome as is the bottle of water. If you are walking a long way round the bank take your wading stick to help you over the terrain and travel as light as you can in similar mode to hill loch fishing. Distance really is the bugbear of big lake fishing and therefore a lot of anglers will choose to go afloat.

Boat Specifics

While a good waterproof jacket is always necessary, boat fishing demands good water-repellent clothing for both upper and lower body. Sitting in jeans in a boat is something I only did once as a wee nipper, never again! One splash of spray never mind rain and you sit in a wet puddle all day and come off chilled to the core in a hugely uncomfortable state. Invest in good quality waterproof trousers if you are going to do a lot of boat angling. In addition you will need an extending handle landing net as it is just not safe to haul the fish of a lifetime up over the prow! A waterproof cushion to sit on eases the aches and pains of being static in the boat all day.

In addition make sure that the bottom of your tackle bag is water-proof as you will find water sloshes about under the duck boards of the boat and soaks everything from the

Tackling up for the large stillwater

base up, sandwiches and spare jersey included! With boat angling you may need a drogue with you especially if the water is open and exposed. Drogues slow the boat down and are indispensable when a slower drift is required. For personal safety you should wear a flotation vest, cold water kills quickly even if you are a strong swimmer. Anglers often do not wear this vital piece of equipment because they say it restricts casting, if that is the case get one of those skinny bar-shaped inflatable 'vests' as these are hardly noticeable. If you are using a motor rather than rowing make sure you have spare petrol or if it is electric that the battery charger is up and running. A spare shear pin for the propeller is also vital. Other odd accoutrements for boats include a bailer and I have seen ghillies carry short lengths of strong bendable metal wire as sometimes the metal pins which secure the rollocks go missing.

TACTICS

The Recce

It is essential that you spend time surveying the contours and curves of a big stillwater. Because of the size of the water, a lot of this will be map based but getting an input of local knowledge by hiring a ghillie or a guide will pay dividends. Whether you are fishing highland or lowland you are going to be confronted by a vast glittering sheet of water and without local input and a degree of reconnoitring you can spend precious time fishing in the wrong place. Check out the map for those promontories, islands, drop offs, channels, weed beds and skerries, anything which breaks up the uniformity of the water might hold trout. Some maps will give contours in depth and observing these is vital in planning your attack. In the deep glacial troughs the trout, other than Ferox which normally require different fishing methods, will be nearer margins rather than in the cold sterile deeps especially early and late in the season. Some large lowland stillwaters can be uniformly shallow and therefore theoretically there is a chance of a trout right across the lake.

Keep a low profile when afloat

Concealment

Shoreline fishing requires a degree of blending-in similar to angling on small stillwaters. When boat fishing it is impossible to be invisible, you are adrift on the surface of the trouts' environment, however you can lessen your presence by keeping a low profile and not standing up in the boat. Standing in boats while on a drift is inadvisable for safety reasons in any case, however many anglers persist in doing it sometimes perversely because they do not take a boat cushion.

Early Season Tactics (March to May)

In truth the main early season strategy for attracting trout on large stillwaters is to fish from the bank rather than the boat. Trout in both highland and lowland waters will tend to be lingering close to the shore to access the best supply of food and shelter. Thus early season bank tactics are the same as those previously mentioned for small stillwaters (see Chapter 14), however distance and/or local rules may dictate you have to go afloat. Early season boat fishing can be a cold and demanding business so choose a clement day and be prepared to abort the mission if the weather changes which it often does with remarkable unpredictability. Wind direction will define your drift but you should plan to keep the boat roughly parallel with or drifting toward the shoreline to take in shallows and any fish harbouring areas. Weed beds may be indistinct early in the year but go for landmark points, islands and skerries. Fish often lie between two points i.e. at the mouth of a bay or inlet and a drift between promontories will often pay dividends. Keep your flies over around 4ft to 10ft of water and cast in toward or parallel with the bank.

Whether boat or bank fishing it is often preferable to use a team of flies. I use two or three but I have seen four or five used especially from the boat. This is one heck of a lot of droppers however and given that it is likely to be windy it could be preferable to go with a low number. Space out the droppers roughly 6ft feet apart and use bright slimline flies such as a Butcher, Dunkeld or Silver Invicta on the point with a bushy Zulu or Kate McLaren on the top dropper. If you use a mid dropper it should be a winged fly like a wet Greenwell's. Just as with small stillwater angling cast across or down wind, keep the rod tip parallel on the medium paced retrieve and then just before lifting off, raise the rod tip and dibble the dropper(s) over the surface. Some anglers will Roll cast after the dibble and this is especially necessary if you are using an intermediate or sunk line. Fishing is at its most productive around mid day, watch out for hatches of midge, lake olives or stonefly and keep fishing when others are lunching.

Geoffrey Bucknall dibbling the top dropper on Loch Watten, Caithness

The mayfly season extends for more than two months in Caithness and Sutherland

The window of opportunity can be brief on big waters in early season but then again some larger than average overwintered trout are the prize so persevere. March and April are not months to be ignored but you do need the right weather.

Mid to Late Season Tactics (May to September)

After the first major daphnia blooms of May the switch is thrown and trout become increasingly active in large stillwaters. With lengthening daylight hours the natural food supply will increase and, depending on the area, there can be profuse hatches of olive, stonefly, sedge, midge, cow dung, bibio and mayfly taking place at their allotted times. Sticklebacks and minnows breed in August and some trout will feed almost exclusively on these fish. Note the mayfly season in the northern Highlands goes on for two months from early June to mid August and that many stillwaters large and small feature this luscious insect. Irish waters are justly famed for their mayfly but the lochs of Caithness and Sutherland should not be forgotten. Trout will now spread out more across the water and if it is a shallow lowland this almost certainly means you will need the boat to access fish out of reach from the shore. Deep waters used for hydro power or as reservoirs can suffer from water height fluctuations and again trout can be driven further offshore in which case the boat is useful in accessing their different adopted territories.

Though some dedicated 'loch stylers' will continue throughout the season with a team of traditional wets on floating line I think there is scope for more flexibility. Dry fly is exceptionally useful when the fish are surface feeding and small nymphs are productive on very sunny days when the trout are lying doggo. Floating lines are the norm but fish which have gone down with the daphnia may require an intermediate line. Go with the flow and adapt accordingly.

Common Questions on Fishing Large Stillwaters

I often find trout come short when I fish droppers, why? Contrary to popular belief the numbers of flies on the cast does not give you more chances. Sometimes you will 'line' and/or distract a trout with a dropper especially when he has fixed one of your team of flies in his eye line. This causes him to pluck nervously rather than take a firm hold of the fly.

Do boat anglers catch more fish than bank anglers? No. Boat anglers may have more opportunities to attract trout especially in the second half of the season however it is down to your own skill. Bank angling allows you the opportunity to go back and have a second cast at a rising fish. On a drift you will have gone past. **Why is it necessary to have long rods for this type of fishing?** Traditional loch style demands rhythmic progress: cast retrieve dibble lift off, cast retrieve dibble lift off. A short rod just does not allow much working of droppers and is generally much harder work.

What is the best time of year for fishing these big waters? Because of the sheer volume of water, food chains can be slower in getting started. May, June, July and September are the favoured months, August less so as it can be a bit dour and the trout go off the feed. Also in the peaty areas of Scotland there is a plague of midges during this month and fishers can be fearfully distracted.

TROUTFISHER'S TOP TIPS FOR FISHING LARGE STILLWATERS

1 If you are boat fishing, safety is a priority. Always take your flotation vest and periodically look behind you, weather changes fast on exposed expanses of water.

2 Loch style fishing is ideal for big waters. Teams of flies are productive but keep the droppers well spaced and be prepared to use only one fly if the trout are being spooked.

3 Don't forget the drogue if boat fishing, drifts need to be purposeful and you need enough time to hunt the fish just as you do when angling off the bank.

The Grey Wulff – top mayfly imitation for large stillwaters

16

THE PERFECT ANGLER

'All rising to great places is by a winding stair'
Francis Bacon

When I read one of my son's school reports recently it said 'working towards' a pass in a particular subject. I like that phrase as it sums up neatly what we are all about – working towards becoming the Perfect Angler. But will we ever reach this illustrious goal? Probably not, for the quarry like the weather is thankfully too unpredictable. Wild trout forever challenge and delight us and it is a steep learning curve to get to the top. Still we can have one heck of a lot of fun trying.

TROUTFISHER'S TIPS FOR 'WORKING TOWARDS' BECOMING THE PERFECT ANGLER

1   Accept that wild trout angling is a lifelong learning experience to be savoured and worked on. If you want instant hits go elsewhere.

2   Start the right way with the help of an instructor especially in casting technique but then be prepared to spend time exploring, experimenting and observing. Often this will be a solitary learning experience but it will enrich your fishing no end. Above all learn from your mistakes.

3   Read and absorb as much about the wild trout, as you can. Fishing is not just casting, it is about pursuing a wild creature and to do so successfully you need to know about his habits and behaviour.

4   Be adaptable in your approach to trout angling especially in your tactics. An inflexible attitude achieves little long term success and the pleasures of learning are lessened considerably.

5   Be magnanimous, accept that failure is quite common in this type of angling.

6   Share your accumulated knowledge and experiences with others especially youngsters who are the life blood of the sport. You often get back more than you give out.

7   Get involved and be informed in matters of fish conservation, both in the practical and the scientific. There are many 'experts' in trout fishing – seek a balanced overall view rather than dogma.

8   Treat your fishing as a big happy adventure not an endurance test.

| *Still working hard towards perfection!*

SELECT BIBLIOGRAPHY

Flies and Fly Tying References

A Dictionary of Trout Flies A. Courtney Williams, A. & C. Black
Flies of Scotland Stan Headley, Merlin Unwin
Matching the Hatch Pat O'Reilly, Swan Hill
The New Illustrated Dictionary of Trout Flies John Roberts, Unwin Paperbacks
Waterside Guide John Goddard, Collins Willow

General References

The Complete Book of Fly Fishing Malcolm Greenhalgh (Ed), Mitchell Beazley
Dark Pools Charles Jardine, Crowood
Fly Fishing Tactics for Brown Trout Geoffrey Bucknall, Swan Hill
A Man May Fish T. C. Kingsmill Moore, Colin Smythe
The Trout W. E. Frost and M. E. Brown, Collins
Trout Wildlife Series Various contributors, Stackpole Books

Historical References

Bright Stream of Memory Geoffrey Bucknall, Swan Hill
Early Scottish Angling Literature Professor N. W. Simmonds, Swan Hill
The Experienced Angler Col. Robert Venables, Antrobus Press
A History of Fly Fishing for Trout John Waller Hills, Barry Shurlock & Co
The Practical Angler W. C. Stewart, A & C Black
Trout Fishing W. Earl Hodgson, A & C Black

USEFUL ADDRESSES

Salmon and Trout Association
Fishmongers Hall,
London Bridge,
London EC4R 9EL

Scottish Anglers National Association
Caledonia Club,
32 Abercromby Place,
Edinburgh EH3 6QE

INDEX